Musical Terms, Symbols and Theory

Also by Michael C. Thomsett

Insurance Dictionary (McFarland, 1989)
Real Estate Dictionary (McFarland, 1988)
Investment and Securities Dictionary (McFarland, 1986)

How to Buy a House, Condo or Co-Op
The Complete Guide to Selling Your Home
Getting Started in Options
Investor Factline
Homeowners Money Management
Fundamentals of Bookkeeping and Accounting
Little Black Book of Business Math
Little Black Book of Budgets and Forecasts
Little Black Book of Business Reports
Little Black Book of Business Letters
Builders Guide to Accounting
Builders Office Manual
Contractors Year-Round Tax Guide
Computers: The Builder's New Tool
Contractors Growth and Profit Guide

Musical Terms, Symbols and Theory

An Illustrated Dictionary

compiled by

Michael C. Thomsett

McFarland & Company, Inc., Publishers
Jefferson, North Carolina, and London

British Library Cataloguing-in-Publication data available

Library of Congress Cataloguing-in-Publication Data

Thomsett, Michael C.
    Musical terms, symbols and theory : an illustrated dictionary / by
Michael C. Thomsett.
        p. cm.
    ISBN 0-89950-392-6 (lib. bdg. : 50# alk. paper) ∞
    1. Music—Terminology. I. Title.
ML108.T46 1989
780′.3—dc20   89-42758
                                                              CIP
                                                              MN

Printed in the United States of America

McFarland & Company, Inc., Publishers
    Box 611, Jefferson, North Carolina 28640

To Dino

Table of Contents

Introduction

This illustrated dictionary is a compilation of terms, theories, instruments, and notation of music.

The field of music is both a complex area of study and a constantly changing art. Its complexity is not limited to the study and performance of music, but extends to the many disciplines and theories, styles, and cultural preferences.

The book is divided into several sections:

Glossary of Terms. This largest section provides fully cross-referenced terms for music theory, instruments, notation, and playing instructions. Included are many foreign words and expressions in common use. Cross-referencing is to other entries in the glossary, in most cases. When the reference is to one of the other sections described below, the reference is given in **boldface.**

Multi-Language Instrument Guide. This handy reference section enables the reader to check names of instruments in five languages: English, Italian, French, German and Spanish.

Illustrated Notation Guide. This section shows the common notation symbols used in musical scores. Look up the symbol, find the name, and refer to the Glossary of Terms for a complete definition.

Scales, Keys and Chords. This final section presents the scales for all major keys, and for all harmonic, melodic and natural minor keys; the key signatures of all major keys; and major, minor, augmented, diminished, and dominant seventh chords for all major keys.

This book is a handy and valuable reference for students and experienced musicians alike, helping readers to understand concepts of theory, converse with others in their field, or review areas studied in the past.

Foreign words and phrases included in this book include the following references:

(It.)	Italian
(Fr.)	French
(G.)	German
(Sp.)	Spanish
(Lt.)	Latin

Glossary of Terms

A

a battula (It.) return to tempo.

a capella (It.) literally, for the chapel, a designation for choral music to be sung without accompaniment. See also *choral.*

a due (It.) two instruments shown on one staff.

a piacere (It.) play freely.

a tempo (It.) return to strict tempo.

abandonné (Fr.) freely, with abandon.

abbandono (It.) freely, with abandon.

abbastanza (It.) enough.

abbreviation notation in shorthand form, instructing performers in the method of play. Abbreviations may include instructions for rests, repeats, tempo, and volume. See also *notation; ornament;* and **Illustrated Notation Guide.**

absolute music a form of music that is not associated with extramusical additions, such as a story line, vocal score, dance or narrative. See also *abstract music; ballet; dance; fugue; sonata; symphony; vocal music.*

absolute pitch the ability to sound or name a musical tone, even when another, related tone has not been sounded. The ability may be natural or, in some instances, developed with experience. See also *perfect pitch; pitch; relative pitch.*

abstract music see *absolute music.*

accelerando (It.) gradually increasing tempo.

accent **(1)** emphasis placed on one note or combination of notes, or upon a beat in each measure. In 3/4 time, for example, the accent is usually placed on the first beat; in 4/4 time, the accent is normally on the first and third beats. When the accent is placed on a weak or a partial beat, it is referred to as syncopation. **(2)** lengthened duration in the sounding of a single note, also called an agogic accent. **(3)** emphasis resulting from a raised pitch, known as a tonic accent. **(4)** a dynamic, as the result of increased volume, also called a dynamic mark. See also *agogic accent; dynamic mark; syncopation; tonic.*

---

accent

---

accentato   (It.) accented.

accentuato   (It.) accentuated.

acciaccatura   (It.) a note sounded with or immediately before another to create a dissonant sound. The note is released immediately upon sounding it, while the other note remains. It is similar to a grace note, with the distinction that the acciaccatura is sounded with instead of immediately before the primary note. This notation is used in keyboard music. See also *dissonance; grace note; notation.*

accidental   an alteration from the normal series of tones in a given key. Accidentals are expressed in one of five ways: sharp, flat, double sharp, double flat, and natural. For example, in the key of D Major, the key signature shows that the C and F are sharps, and the rest of the notes are naturals. Any deviation from this key constitutes an accidental. See also *double flat; double sharp; flat; key signature; natural; sharp;* and **Scales, Keys and Chords.** See illustration, page 3.

accolade   a brace or bar indicating a grouping together of instruments or voices. See also *bar line; brace.*

accompaniment   the music supporting a melody, primary performer or instrument, to supply flavor, a bass line, chords for tonal identity, or rhythm. See also *melody; orchestration; rhythm.*

accordeon   (It.) see *accordion.*

accordéon   (Fr.) see *accordion.*

accordion   a hand-held keyboard instrument with two headboards and a bellows. As the bellows is compressed and expanded, air causes metal reeds to

accidental

sharp	♯
flat	♭
double sharp	✗
double flat	♭♭
natural	♮

vibrate and create sound. A keyboard on the right-hand headboard is used to modify those vibrations and create individual tones or tones in combination. A series of buttons on the left-hand headboard creates bass tones and chords. See also *chord; concertina; keyboard instrument.*

acordeón   (Sp.) see *accordion.*

acoustics   the study of sound, including quality, intervals, overtones and sound properties of structures and instruments. See also *interval; just intonation; overtone; pitch.*

action   a device on a musical instrument operated by hands or feet to produce, modify or control sound. For example, keys and their connected parts are the action on keyboard instruments. A harp's action is controlled by the feet. And action on woodwinds consists of levers that open or close air holes. See also *keyboard; woodwind.*

ad libitum   (Lt.) at will.

adagietto   (It.) somewhat faster than adagio.

adagio   (It.) slowly.

adagissimo   (It.) very slowly.

adaptation   an arrangement or variation of the work of another composer. It is different from a transcription, which is usually faithful to the intent of the original music. An adaptation may change the tone, emphasis or harmony. See also *arrangement; orchestration; transcription.*

added sixth chord   a chord consisting of the tonic (first), mediant (third) and dominant (fifth) notes, plus the submediant (sixth). Thus, the triad of 1-3-5 is extended to 1-3-5-6. An added sixth applies either to a major or minor key. For example, in the key of G Major, the added sixth consists of G, B, D and E. In the key of G Minor, the chord is made up of G, B flat, D and E. See also *chord; dominant; major interval; mediant; minor interval; submediant; tonic; triad.*

added sixth chord

major   minor

additional accompaniment   the addition of orchestration, voice, or other changes to the score of a composition. This may improve upon the original, or it may change the mood, rhythm, or intention of the composer. See also *accompaniment; melody; orchestration; rhythm.*

aeolian harp   an ancient instrument containing several strings, all tuned identically, but consisting of different textures and thickness. When exposed to wind, various harmonics result. See also *harmonics; string family.*

Aeolian mode   also known as the natural minor scale, the white notes of the piano, beginning and ending with A. See also *authentic mode; Church modes; diatonic; modality; natural minor scale; Plagal mode.*

Aeolian mode

aerophone   any instrument on which sound is produced by a column of vibrating air. See also *accordion; brass family; organ; pipe; wind family.*

affettuoso   (It.) affectionately.

affretando   (It.) hurried.

after-beat **(1)** weak beats in a measure, or notes connecting more strongly emphasized notes. **(2)** grace notes and other ornaments, added at the end of a trill or as optional notes. See also *grace note; ornament; trill.*

agitato (It.) agitated.

agité (Fr.) agitated.

agogic accent an accent resulting from the holding of a note or a series of notes for a longer beat than usual. Notation for this accent is given in scores by way of the fermata (pause). See also *accent; fermata; notation.*

air (Fr.) a melody or tune, often used as the title of a short aria or simple composition with an especially strong melody. See also *aria; melody; tune.*

al fine (It.) to the end.

al segno (It.) at the sign.

Alberti bass a pattern of bass accompaniment used extensively in 18th century compositions, named for Domenico Alberti, a composer who applied the technique for bass lines in many keyboard sonatas. The line may vary, but is typically identified by a series of quarter notes in a distinct 1-5-3-5 pattern. See also *accompaniment; bass; sonata; texture.*

Alberti bass

---

aleatory music a form of music in which the composer leaves some elements or interpretations to the discretion of the performer. See also *chance music.*

aliquot tone a tone above one that is sounded, also called a harmonic, overtone or partial tone. See also *harmonic series; overtone; partial.*

alla breve (It.) quick duple time, with the half note on the beat, rather than the quarter note (2/2 in place of 4/4 time). The instruction is represented by a special time signature mark. See also *duple meter; notation; time signature.* See illustration, page 6.

allargando (It.) slower and louder.

allegretto (It.) quickly.

alla breve

---

allegro   (It.) very quickly.

allemande   (Fr.) a dance typically in 4/4 time as used by Baroque era composers; or in 3/4 time in most classical music examples. See also *Baroque; classical; dance.*

allentando   (It.) slowing tempo.

alt.   abbrevation derived from the word 'alto,' indicating a higher range. This is used to indicate notes are to be sounded above the treble clef, even when written within the clef's range. See also *range; treble clef.*

alteration   a change of one chromatic step up or down. For example, a note can be raised (natural to sharp, sharp to double sharp, or flat to natural); or it can be lowered (natural to flat, flat to double flat, or sharp to natural). See also *accidental; chromatic scale.*

altered chord   a change in a chord of one or more notes by way of increasing or decreasing by one chromatic step. See also *accidental; augmented chord; chord; diminished chord; triad.*

alto   (It.) high; a female voice range lower than soprano, also called contralto. See also *contralto; voice.*

---

alto

average range

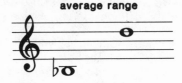

---

alto clef   a clef used for viola parts, with the center emphasizing the middle of five lines on the staff. That line is keyed as Middle C. The identical symbol is used in vocal music on occasion, and may indicate a different location for

Middle C. In that instance, the symbol is referred to as the tenor clef. See also *clef; range; tenor clef; viola.*

---

alto clef

---

alto saxophone a saxophone that sounds one major sixth below the written score, properly called the E flat alto saxophone. See also *saxophone.*

---

alto saxophone

written   sounded

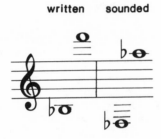

---

alto trombone an instrument that filled out the upper range of the trombone family, before the value trumpet became popular. In modern scores, a second tenor trombone takes the place previously held by the alto trombone, with higher note ranges given to trumpet parts. The alto's pitch is a perfect fourth above the tenor trombone. See also *tenor trombone; trombone; trumpet.*

alzati (It.) remove mutes from strings.

amabile (It.) amiably.

Ambrosian chant a form of liturgical chant named for St. Ambrose, also called plainsong. The Ambrosian chant is believed to be the source of the antiphonal singing form. See also *antiphon; chant; Gregorian chant; plainsong.*

amoroso (It.) tenderly.

amplitude the range of a sound wave, from its highest to its lowest point. See also *range.*

ancora (It.) again.

andante (It.) moderate speed.

andantino (It.) faster than andante.

anfang (G.) from the beginning.

anglaise (Fr.) a song or movement in a suite, in the style of an English dance. See also *dance; suite.*

Anglican chant musical form derived from the four-part harmony developed during the 16th century and practiced in Anglican church music. See also *chant; harmony.*

animato (It.) animated.

animé (Fr.) animated.

anschwellen (G.) increase volume.

answer **(1)** also called the consequent, the response section of a fugue, appearing as the second and fourth voices. A real answer imitates the original subject exactly, but is usually written a perfect fifth above. A tonal answer is one that is somewhat modified in respect of the key and to preserve tonal quality. **(2)** the section of a canon that imitates the primary melody. See also *antiphon; canon; consequent; contrapuntal; fugue; imitation; real answer; subject; tonal answer.*

---

answer

antecedent   in the introductory section of a fugue, the subject, or primary theme. It is imitated or repeated by the consequent (answer). See also *consequent; exposition; fugue; subject.*

anthem   a vocal composition accompanied by organ in Anglican church tradition; also widely used to describe any solemn, religious or patriotic composition. See also *choral; organ; vocal music.*

anticipation   the sounding of a single note in advance of the remainder of its chord. This creates a nonharmonic tone that is resolved upon sounding the rest of the chord. See also *chord; dissonance; nonharmonic tone; resolution.*

---

anticipation

---

antiphon   meaning cross or counter sounding, a style of chorus singing involving alternating vocal groups. In Gregorian chants, the antiphon was a short text sung before and after a canticle. The term also refers to the repeating of a section one octave above the first chorus, as a form of answer. See also *answer; chant; chorus; Gregorian chant; octave; vocal music.*

aperto   (It.) open, not muted, an instruction for brass instruments. See also *brass family; mute.*

appassionato   (It.) passionately.

appoggiatura   (It.) a "leaning" note, an ornament or grace note, most often a major second above the note immediately following. It generally is not assigned a measure value, and may be shown as a small note in one of three forms:
  (a) with a short stem,
  (b) with a stem and diagonal stroke, or
  (c) with a connecting tie.
See also *grace note; nonharmonic tone; ornament.* See illustration, page 10.

appoggiatura

---

arabesque (Fr.) title of a short composition containing decorative or highly ornamental qualities. See also *form; ornamentation.*

arch form a form of composition in which sections are repeated in reverse order after their introduction. It differs from the rondo form, in which themes alternate (theme A, then B, then A, or ABA form). An arch form consists of themes played in ABCBA order. See also *form; rondo form.*

arco (It.) instruction to stringed instruments to play with the bow. See also *bow; pizzicato; string family.*

aria (It.) a complex vocal solo, traditionally part of an opera. The aria may be included primarily to demonstrate a singer's vocal abilities, rather than to further the story of the opera. See also *air; de capo aria; opera; solo; song; vocal music.*

arietta (It.) a simplified aria. See also *opera; vocal music.*

arioso (It.) expressively.

armonica (It.) see *harmonica.*

armónica (Sp.) see *harmonica.*

armonio (Sp.) see *harmonium.*

arpa (It.) (Sp.) see *harp.*

arpeggio (It.) a chord played one note at a time, in quick succession, as in the style associated with harp music. The notation consists of
(a) a wavy line,
(b) ornamental notes, or
(c) a vertical bow.
See also *broken chord; chord; notation; ornament.* See illustration, page 11.

arpeggione a guitar-shaped instrument with six strings, played with a bow, now obsolete. See also *guitar; string family; violin.*

arpeggio

---

arrangement   an adaption of a work to a different instrument or combination of instruments than as originally composed. For example, a vocal composition may be orchestrated for a string quartet; or a simple orchestral piece may be expanded to a more complex form. An arrangement is usually faithful to the original composer's intention, as opposed to a transcription, in which variations or elaborations may be added. See also *adaptation; orchestration; transcription.*

ars antiqua   (Lt.) the old art, descriptive of music of the 13th century. The primary form of music during this period was the motet, and standards were established for composition in rhythmic modes. One- and two-part vocal music was expanded, and the concept of polyphony was introduced. See also *monophonic sound; motet; polyphony; rhythmic mode.*

ars nova   (Lt.) the new art, music as practiced during the 14th century. Popular forms included the motet, with significant development of polyphonic forms. Music written in duple meter gained in popularity during this period. See also *duple meter; motet; polyphony.*

art song   a serious composition for voice, including accompaniment, distinguished from the less formal folk song. See also *accompaniment; folk music; song; vocal music.*

articulation   the method of performing a note or series of notes. The two major forms of articulation are legato and staccato. See also *legato; staccato.*

assai   (It.) fast.

atonal music   music that purposely avoids an identity with a specific key. All 12 tones are assigned equal value and importance, and generally accepted rules of tonality and key relationships do not apply. Atonal compositions are written in the 12-tone system, although not all 12-tone music is atonal. See also *chromaticism; key; tonality; twelve-tone music.*

attaca   (It.) proceed without pause.

attack   the method of introducing or sounding a note or series of notes. See also *note.*

augmentation **(1)** doubling or tripling the performance speed of a section, a technique used in many fugues. Speed may also be reduced, a process known as diminution. **(2)** to increase the orchestration or performance voices, adding power, sound quality or elaboration. **(3)** the raising of a note by one half step. See also *diminution; fugue; half step; interval; orchestration.*

augmented chord a chord containing one or more notes raised a half step. Any note in a triad can be raised, although reference to an augmented chord usually refers to the raised fifth (dominant). Thus, a C augmented chord contains the notes C, E and G sharp. See also *chord; half step; interval;* and **Scales, Keys and Chords.**

augmented chord

authentic cadence a series of chords ending with a tonic triad that is preceded by a chord with the dominant note in the bass. The authentic cadence includes a final chord with the tonic in top and bottom positions. See also *cadence; chord; dominant; half cadence; imperfect cadence; perfect cadence; tonic; triad.*

authentic cadence

authentic mode   descriptive of a Church mode beginning and ending on the final (today called the tonic). In comparison, a Plagal mode begins a fourth below the final. For example, the Phrygian mode in authentic form begins and ends on E. The related Plagal form, also called the hypophrygian mode, begins and ends on B. See also *Church modes; final; mode; Plagal mode; tonic.*

auxiliary tone   a tone sounded in a series that, by itself, would be dissonant with the chord being sounded in accompaniment. However, it is acceptable in relation to the notes sounded before and after the auxiliary tone. See also *harmony; nonharmonic tone; tone.*

---

auxiliary tone

---

ayre   a homophonic style of song, popular in the 17th century. It consists of a melody accompanied by other instruments or by voices. See also *air; homophonic sound; song.*

B

back beat   a style of rhythm in which the emphasis is placed in unusual beats. For example, in 4/4 time, the second and fourth beats are accented rather than the first and third. See also *beat; pop; rhythm; syncopation.*

badinage   (Fr.) a composition or dance written in a light or playful style. See also *dance.*

bagatelle   (Fr.) a short composition for piano. See also *character piece; piano.*

bagpipe   an instrument consisting of reed pipes and a bag. The pipes are divided into two categories. Chanter pipes include finger holes and produce the melody. Drones are for bass accompaniment, and sound unchanging tones. The Scottish variety's bag is filled with air from the player's mouth, and the Irish bagpipe produces sound by way of a bellows held under the player's arm. See also *chanter; drone; reed; wind family.*

balalaika a Russian instrument similar to the guitar. It has a triangular body and a long neck divided into frets. Most forms of the instrument have three strings, divided by perfect fourth intervals. See also *guitar; string family.*

balance the relationship of various instruments or sections to one another, in terms of dominance or combined dynamic quality. See also *orchestration.*

ballad a composition combined with a narrative, originally a dance with a related story line. The term has evolved over time to include music descriptive of adverturous or romantic tales. See also *dance; folk music; song.*

ballad opera a form of production combining folk music and dialogue, either spoken or sung. This form was popular in 18th century English music. See also *folk music; opera; song.*

ballade (Fr.) a poem set to music, which originated in the 13th century; an instrumental interpretation of a poetic work. See also *art song; song.*

ballet a dramatic presentation combining story and dance with orchestral music, which evolved from 16th century court dances celebrating special occasions. See also *dance; opera ballet.*

ballo (It.) dance.

band an instrumental ensemble consisting of several types of instruments, most often brass, woodwind and percussion. When stringed instruments are added, the ensemble is usually referred to as an orchestra. See also *brass band; ensemble; instrumentation; orchestra.*

banjo an American stringed instrument used in pop and folk music. The body is a thin drum, and either five or six strings are divided into frets. It is plucked like the guitar. See also *folk music; guitar; pop; string family.*

bar line a line drawn from the top to the bottom of the staff to indicate the division of measures. See also *measure.*

---

bar line

barbershop   a style of vocal music using close harmony, notably diminished, augmented and added sixth chords. See also *close harmony; harmony; song; vocal music.*

barcarole   "boat song," typically written in 6/8 time, originating with the music sung by gondoliers in Venice. See also *song.*

bariolage   (Fr.) an effect used in violin music, in which two strings are played alternatively. Harmonics are sounded from the lower string, or a form of tremolo results. See also *broken chord; harmonics; tremolo; violin.*

bariolage

0   4   0   4

baritone   the middle range of a male voice, between tenor and bass. See also *bass; tenor; voice.*

baritone

average range

baritone saxophone   properly called the E flat baritone, this instrument sounds one octave and a major sixth interval below the notes as written. See also *brass family; saxophone.* See illustration, page 16.

Baroque   descriptive of music composed after the Renaissance and before the classical periods. The Baroque period extends from approximately 1600 to 1750. Most significant among developments during this period were the theory and practice of the thorough bass. Prominent composers of Baroque music

baritone saxophone

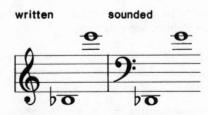

include Bach and Handel. See also *classical; Renaissance music; thorough bass.*

basic set the 12 tones contained within a single octave, a term used in the 12-tone technique. See also *atonal music; series; twelve-tone music.*

bass **(1)** the lowest male voice, lower than tenor and baritone. **(2)** the lowest part in an arrangement of two or more voices or instruments. See also *baritone; tenor; voice.*

bass

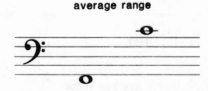

bass clarinet more accurately called the bass clarinet in B flat, an instrument that is used to provide the bass part in a woodwind section, with or in place of the bassoon. It is a transposing instrument, with actual sound a major second interval below the written note. See also *clarinet; wind family.* See illustration, page 17.

bass clef the clef used in orchestral music for the bass line, also called the F clef. The two periods of the clef indicate that the second line from the top of the staff represents the note F. The line notes (from bottom to top) are G, B, D, F and A. Space note values (from bottom to top) are A, C, E, and G. See also *clef; treble clef.* See illustration, page 17.

bass drum a drum of indefinite pitch, placed in an upright position so that either skin can be struck. Orchestral bass drums measure from 24 to 36 inches

bass clarinet

bass clef

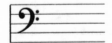

in diameter, and band bass drums may be as large as 40 inches. The bass drumstick is wooden, with a softened felt knob. Rolls are achieved with the use of tympani sticks. Bass drum parts are written on an indefinite pitch clef. See also *drum; indefinite pitch clef; percussion family.*

bass fiddle   see *double bass.*

bass saxophone   properly called the B flat bass saxophone, actual sound is two octaves and a major second below the written note. See also *brass family; saxophone.* See illustration, page 18.

bass trombone   lowest ranging instrument in the trombone group, more accurately called the tenor-bass trombone. The sounded and written notes are identical. See also *brass family; trombone.* See illustration, page 18.

bass trumpet   instrument that sounds a major ninth interval below the written note. In most scores, this range is assigned to the trombone. The bass trumpet is used when the greater resonance of a trumpet is desired in the lower range. See also *brass family; trumpet.* See illustration, page 18.

bass viol   see *double bass.*

bass saxophone

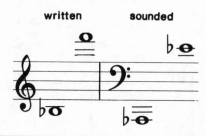

bass trombone

bass trumpet

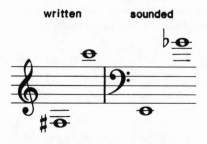

basse danse (Fr.) a "low dance," probably a reference to the style of sliding rather than lifting the feet, evolved from 16th century France. See also *dance*.

basset horn a low-ranging form of the clarinet, whose parts are often played by the alto or bass clarinet. This instrument was used prominently by Mozart. See also *bass clarinet; clarinet; wind family*.

bassethorn (G.) see *basset horn*.

basso continuo (It.) see *thorough bass.*

basson (Fr.) see *bassoon.*

bassoon the bass instrument of the wind family, capable of playing a wide range of notes two octaves below the oboe. It sounds the same pitch as written. See also *oboe; wind family.*

bassoon

battery descriptive of the percussion section of an orchestra. See also *percussion family.*

battuta (It.) return to strict tempo.

beam the line connecting partial count notes into groupings. See also **Illustrated Notation Guide.**

beam

beat the pulse of music as directed by the combination of tempo and meter signatures. For example, an allegro in 4/4 time calls for four fast beats per measure. And a largo is 3/4 time indicates three slow beats per measure. See also *down beat; meter; tempo; up beat.*

bebop jazz style developed in the United States during the 1940s, involving solo or group improvisation, syncopation, and extended harmony, with 12-measure blues phrasing. See also *improvisation; jazz.*

becken (G.) see *cymbal.*

bel a unit of sound. One-tenth of a bel is a decibel, the lowest degree of change in loudness that can be identified by ear. See also *decibel.*

bel canto (It.) "beautiful song," a style of agility and ease in vocal music, most often associated with operatic singing. See also *opera; song; vocal music.*

bell a percussion instrument constructed of metal alloys, sounded by clapper or hammer. See also *percussion family.*

bells reference to chimes, glockenspiel and other metallic percussion instruments with definite pitch. See also *percussion family; pitch.*

belly the top surface of stringed instruments, that part of the body directly beneath the strings. See also *string family.*

bémol (Fr.) flat.

bemolle (It.) flat.

berceuse (Fr.) a lullaby. See also *song.*

binary form music with two distinct sections. These sections may be of equal or unequal length, with the first part repeated after introduction and development of the second. The binary form evolved into the sonata form after the 18th century. See also *compound binary form; sonata form; ternary form.*

bitonality a composition style in which two keys are played together, sometimes called polytonality. Bitonality differs from atonality, which is the intentional avoidance of key identity. See also *atonal music; polytonality; tonality.*

blind octave a devise used for piano music, in which octave intervals are played in quick succession by both hands. This is intended to demonstrate the virtuosity of the performer. See also *piano.* See illustration, page 21.

bloc de bois (Fr.) see *wood block.*

blocco di legno (It.) see *wood block.*

block chords simplified style of accompaniment consisting of a triad of chords, without arrangement for a figured bass or concern with tonic and dominant support. See also *accompaniment; broken chord; figured bass.* See illustration, page 21.

blockflöte (G.) see *recorder.*

blue notes diminished third and seventh notes in a scale (and at times, the fifth note), so called because the resulting chords are typical in blues music. See also *diminished chord.* See illustration, page 21.

blind octave

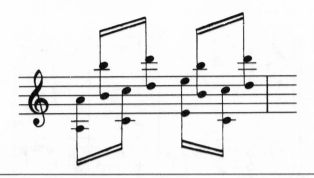

block chords

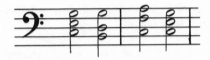

blue notes

blues a 20th century vocal and instrumental style of music characterized by diminished third and seventh tones and, occasionally, by diminished fifth tones; and by 12-measure statements rather than the traditional 16 bars associated with western music. See also *jazz; rhythm.*

bolero a Spanish dance in 3/4 time, often accompanied by drums, castanets and other percussion instruments. Rhythms set by way of a triplet in the second and third beats of the bass line are common. See also *dance; triplet.* See illustration, page 22.

bongo a small drum shaped like a bucket, played with the fingers and palms, that may or may not have definite pitch. See also *drum; percussion family.*

bolero

boogie-woogie a style of jazz piano music in which the rhythm is set by repeated (ostinato) bass, often with a free or improvised right hand part. See also *broken chord; jazz; ostinato; piano.*

bore the diameter of the inside of a brass or wind instrument. The depth, width and shape of the bore and type of mouthpiece used will affect the tone color of a performance. See also *mouthpiece; tone color.*

bouché (Fr.) stopped (brass instruments).

bourrée (Fr.) a French dance of the 17th century, usually with an emphasis on the fourth beat in 4/4 time. See also *dance.*

bow a stick used for playing stringed instruments. Horse hairs are strung between the tip and the base (the frog), which causes strings to vibrate as the bow is moved across them. See also *frog; nut; string family.*

bowing the method of producing sound on a stringed instrument, using a bow. The notation "arco" is given to instruct the performer to return to bowing following a pizzacato (plucked) section. The two common bowing methods are legato (smoothly) and staccato (short, hammered notes). See also *arco; down-bow; legato; pizzicato; staccato; string family; up-bow.*

brace a connecting bracket used to show that two staves are played together, as are a treble and bass clef part for the piano. See also **Illustrated Notation Guide.** See illustration, page 23.

brass band a band ensemble made up of brass and percussion instruments. See also *band; ensemble.*

brace

---

brass family   instruments constructed of metal, with cupped mouthpieces. The most popular orchestral brass instruments are horn, trumpet, trombone and tuba. In addition, bands may employ the cornet, saxophone, and a range of other brass instruments, often in a wide variety of playing ranges. See also *horn; orchestration; trombone; trumpet; tuba.*

bratsche   (G.) see *viola.*

break   **(1)** a pause in a score calling for complete silence or silence in one instrument or section. **(2)** a change in tonal quality resulting when an instrument or voice moves from one register to another. See also *notation; register.*

breve   British term for a double whole note, or a whole note held for two measures. See also *notation; whole note.*

---

breve

---

bridge   part of a stringed instrument that raises the strings above the wood, so that vibrations can be created and sent to the body of the instrument. See also *string family.*

bridge passage   a section of a composition that connects two other sections or movements. The bridge passage may be used for transition from one theme to another, or to modulate to a different key. See also *modulation.*

brio   (It.) energy.

broken chord   performance of a chord with notes played in rhythmic sequence or as an arpeggio, rather than as a block chord. See also *Alberti bass; arpeggio; block chords.*

---

broken chord

---

bugle   a brass instrument without valves, capable of sounding notes in only one harmonic series. See also *brass family; harmonic series; valve.*

C

cabaletta   (It.) operatic song used as the closing section of arias and duets. See also *aria; duet; opera; song.*

cacophony   the use of dissonance to intentionally create a harsh mood or tone to music. See also *dissonance.*

cadence   the closing section of a phrase, involving two or more chords. A perfect cadence consists of a dominant chord, followed by a tonic, with the root in both top and bottom voices. A deceptive cadence is one in which the expected tonic resolution does not occur. A different chord follows the dominant. See also *authentic cadence; deceptive cadence; feminine cadence; masculine cadence; perfect cadence.*

cadenza   a section of concertos or arias intended to be improvised by the performer, to show virtuosity. See also *aria; concerto; improvisation.*

calando   (It.) softer and slower.

calliope   an American instrument developed in the late 19th century, constructed of a series of whistles played by a keyboard. See also *keyboard instrument.*

calore   (It.) warmth.

cambia   (It.) change instruments.

cambiata tones   nonharmonic tones occurring between chords or other notes, and not part of the rhythm of the music. The cambiata tone moves toward the resolution note. See also *nonharmonic tone; resolution; rhythm.*

cambiata tones

camera   music intended to be played in a small room, as opposed to compositions for the church. See also *Baroque; chamber music.*

Camerata   a late 16th century group of artists, musicians and writers who devised the concept of expressing drama in musical forms. These meetings and discussions are credited with the early development of opera. See also *opera.*

campanas   (Sp.) see *bells.*

campane   (It.) see *bells.*

campanelli   (It.) see *glockenspiel.*

cancel   the removal of an accidental instruction, by placing a natural in its place. See also *accidental.*

cancel

cancrizans the presentation of a theme, first in original sequence and then in exactly the reverse order. See also *counter fugue; inversion; mirror fugue.*

cancrizans

canon a form of counterpoint music involving the strict imitation of a theme in two or more voices. See also *counterpoint; imitation; perpetual canon; round; voice.*

cantabile (It.) in singing style.

cantata a Baroque form of non-dramatic vocal and instrumental music. The cantata contains four or more movements, including arias, duets, and choruses. The form derives from secular monodic music, and was expanded by Bach for use in church compositions. See also *Baroque; monody.*

canticle that section of the church liturgy that involves singing rather than speaking parts. See also *chant; vocal music.*

cantus firmus (Lt.) fixed song; a theme that is expanded with the addition of counterpoint voices. The form originated with elaborated compositions based on Gregorian chants. See also *counterpoint; Gregorian chant; polyphony; song.*

canzona (It.) a lyrical song or short instrumental composition written in song style. See also *song.*

canzonet a short, light song. See also *song.*

capo a device attached to depress a guitar's strings and reduce the playable number of frets, thus changing the open-string note value and key. See also *guitar; key relationship.*

capriccio (It.) a light or humorous instrumental piece written in fugue form. See also *fugue.*

caramillo (Sp.) see *flageolet.*

carillon   a chromatically tuned set of bells played mechanically, by way of a remote keyboard connected by wires. See also *keyboard instrument*.

carol   originally a dance song, a vocal composition associated with religious celebration. See also *dance; folk music; song; vocal music*.

cascabeles   (Sp.) see *sleigh bells*.

cassation   a composition for small instrumental groups, developed in the 18th century. See also *divertimento; orchestra*.

castagnette   (It.) see *castanets*.

castagnettes   (Fr.) see *castanets*.

castanets   a percussion instrument consisting of two small wooden shells that are held together by string. The string is attached to the performer's fingers, and the two shells are struck together to produce a sharp, rhythmic sound. See also *percussion family; rhythm*.

castañueles   (Sp.) see *castanets*.

castrato   (It.) a male soprano whose vocal range and quality was preserved by castration, a practice in 17th and 18th century Italy. See also *soprano; vocal music*.

catch   a round popular in 17th and 18th century England, often of a humorous or ribald nature. See also *round; vocal number*.

cavatina   (It.) a slow song in an opera, or a slow movement in a string quartet. See also *opera; song; string quartet*.

celesta   a keyboard instrument with a four-octave range beginning at middle C. A hammer strikes metal bars to produce a crisp bell-like tone. See also *keyboard instrument*.

---

celesta

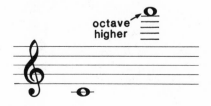

cello   one of four popular stringed instruments (the other three being the violin, viola and double bass), played with a bow. The performer sits and bows across the upright instrument while it rests on an adjustable pin. Open strings are C (two octaves below middle C), G, D and A. See also *string family; violoncello.*

---

cello

---

cembalo   (G.) see *harpsichord.*

cent   one hundredth of a half tone, used for the precise measurement of musical intervals. See also *interval; semitone.*

chaconne   a composition of the Baroque period, in which a theme is introduced and then subjected to a series of harmonies and tonal variations. See also *Baroque; theme.*

chaleur   (Fr.) warmth.

chamber music   music performed by small ensembles of instruments, each having equal importance and singular parts. In comparison, orchestral music includes parts that are doubled by several sections in the group. Chamber music is intended to be played in a room (or chamber), as opposed to music meant for a church or theater. See also *ensemble; instrumentation.*

chamber opera   an opera performed with a limited or small instrumental ensemble, and with a small number of performers. See also *ensemble; opera.*

chamber orchestra   an ensemble consisting of a limited number of instruments, each playing a part by itself. Chamber orchestras are usually limited to woodwinds and strings. See also *ensemble; instrumentation; string family; wind family.*

chance music   see *aleatory music.*

change ringings   a form of music popularized in England, in which a group of performers executes various melodies and combinations of tones. Each person rings one bell only. The possible number of changes (combinations) increases with the number of performers. See also *ensemble; percussion family.*

chanson   a French song that developed into multiple-part polyphonic songs of the 16th century, similar to the madrigal of other countries. See also *madrigal; polyphony; song; vocal music.*

chant   a song in monophonic style and without a specific rhythm. See also *Ambrosian chant; Anglican chant; Gregorian chant; monophonic sound; song.*

chanter   one of two pipes in the bagpipe, containing finger holes that are opened and closed to produce the melody. See also *bagpipe.*

character piece   descriptive of music written primarily for piano during the 19th century. They are generally shorter and less developed than more formalized compositions, such as symphonies and sonatas. Character pieces convey a mood rather than thorough development, and include titles such as bagatelle, intermezzo, impromptu, etude, nocturne, and fantasy. See also *piano.*

chart   the arrangement of pop or jazz music. See also *arrangement; jazz; pop.*

chimes   a percussion instrument, usually 18 hanging bells that are struck with a hammer to produce bell tones. See also *bells; percussion family.*

chimes

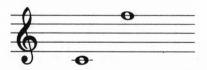

Chinese block   hollow wooden blocks that are struck with a drumstick, also called the temple block. This instrument is used in jazz bands. See also *jazz; percussion family; temple block; wood block.*

chironomy   a conducting style specifically applied to non-rhythmic forms of music, notably Gregorian chants. See also *chant; conduct; Gregorian chant.*

chitarra   (It.) see *guitar.*

chiuso (It.) a direction in horn music, for a muted or stopped effect. See also *horn; mute; stopped.*

choir (1) a group of singers, associated with the vocal portion of church music. (2) a section of one, specific family of instruments in a larger orchestra, used in place of "section." (3) an abbreviated name for the choir organ. (4) one of the manuals on the organ. (5) the part of a church where singers are located, also called the choir loft. See also *band; chorus; orchestral score; vocal music.*

choir organ a small, limited range organ designed to accompany a choir; or, a manual of a larger organ intended to accompany vocal music. See also *keyboard instrument; organ.*

choral any form of music intended to by sung by a choir, or in general, a vocal section of a composition. See also *vocal music.*

choral symphony a symphony utilizing only vocal parts or, in more its more common application, an instrumental symphony that includes a choir section. See also *symphony; vocal music.*

chorale (1) a form of hymn popularized during the development of the early Protestant church in Germany. (2) word used as part of the title of some vocal music. See also *hymn; song; vocal music.*

chorale cantata a highly structured form of chorale in cantata form. See also *cantata; vocal music.*

chorale prelude a composition for organ, played as part of a church service. It usually immediately precedes the singing of a chorale. See also *organ; prelude.*

chord (1) the sounding of three or more notes at the same time, to identify the key, interval relationships, development and texture of music. (2) to chord, the process of adding harmony to a melody line. See also *altered chord; consonance; dissonance; harmony; interval; texture; tone cluster; triad;* and **Scales, Keys and Chords.**

chord range notes in a range beginning about one octave below middle C, through the F above middle C. This range is considered ideal for the playing of chords. Below this range, close harmony is not clear enough to create acceptable tonal quality. And above this section is the melody range. See also *melody range; middle C; range.* See illustration, page 31.

chord symbol (1) an abbreviated form of instrumentation used in pop music, especially for guitar and piano performance or accompaniment. A chord symbol is written above the melody line, either in place of an accompaniment or in addition to it. The symbol does not state the formation of the chord. For example, a series of chord symbols above a melody line reads:

    C   G7   C   Cdim   F   G7   C

chord range

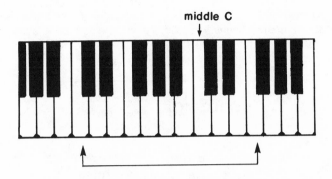

middle C

---

(2) alternative method of chording for guitar music, involving a grid printed above the melody line, with an abbreviated chord symbol above. Each row of grid spaces from left to right represents one fret on the guitar. Each line from top to bottom represents the guitar strings. Open strings are indicated with a small, unfilled circle above the last fret line. Strings that are not to be played at all have no symbols. Strings to be depressed are indicated with a black circle on the appropriate line (string) and in the appropriate row (fret). See also *guitar; pop.*

---

chord symbol

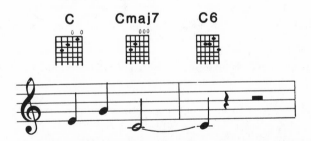

C   Cmaj7   C6

---

chordal style an arrangement made up of chords. In strict chordal style, the number of parts does not vary. For example, four voices are used to create four-note chords throughout. In free chordal style, the number of parts will vary for each chord. See also *composition; instrumentation.*

chording **(1)** the inclusion of a chord symbol (the abbreviated chord name plus a grid) to instruct a performer in performance of a song; to indicate the preferred method of performance; or to teach a beginning player how to perform a chord. In the latter case, the simplest method of forming a chord is given, while a more experienced player might prefer an advanced version of the same chord for improved tonal quality, balance, and integrity of sound. **(2)** the spacing of intervals in a chord, a term used to judge the quality of sound. Example: close intervals in the bass range will not produce as clear a sound as will wider interval arrangements. Removing the mediant from a deep bass part, and placing the tonic in the top position of the chord will clarify tonal quality. See also *accompaniment; guitar; interval; piano.*

---

chording

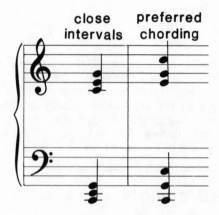

choreographic poem   a composition written for performance as part of a ballet or other dramatic dance. See also *ballet; dance; symphonic poem.*

choreography   the direction and planning of ballet and other dramatic dance. See also *ballet; dance; modern dance.*

chorus   **(1)** a choir or group of singers performing in vocal parts. **(2)** the refrain of a song. **(3)** a grouping of instruments in an orchestra, or sections of similar or identical instruments playing the same part. See also *choir; instrumentation; refrain; song; vocal music.*

chromatic scale   a scale based on all 12 notes in an octave. See also *diatonic; note; octave; scale.* See illustration, page 33.

chromaticism   music employing semitone progressions, augmented and diminished chords, and other combinations outside of the traditional diatonic scale. The term "chroma" is derived from the Greek for color, and is used to describe the addition of color, variety and drama to a composition. Chromatic variations often are employed to develop a theme, or as a device to add emotional effect. See also *altered chord; diatonic; harmony; semitone.*

chromatic scale

Church modes   modes utilizing only the white keys of a piano, used for music prior to the 17th century. In modern music, Church modes have been replaced with the major and the minor modes.

Church modes before the 16th century were limited to four types: Dorian, Phrygian, Lydian and Mixolydian. These modes began on D, E, F and G. The system was later expanded to include the Aeolian and Ionian modes, starting on notes A and C. The Locrian mode, beginning on B, is a theoretical mode only, since it includes a diminished fifth interval, making it impractical for tonal applications. See also *Aeolian mode; authentic mode; Dorian mode; Ionian mode; Locrian mode; Lydian mode; Mixolydian mode; Phrygian mode; Plagal mode.* See illustration, page 34.

circle of fifths   a visual representation of all the major keys, arranged in ascending and descending fifths. The circle shows the mathematical logic of keys, progressive notation, and relationships:

key	number of sharps	Key	number of flats
C	0		
G	1		
D	2		
A	3		
E	4		
B	5	C♭	7
F♯	6	G♭	6
C♯	7	D♭	5
		A♭	4
		E♭	3
		B♭	2
		F	1
		C	0

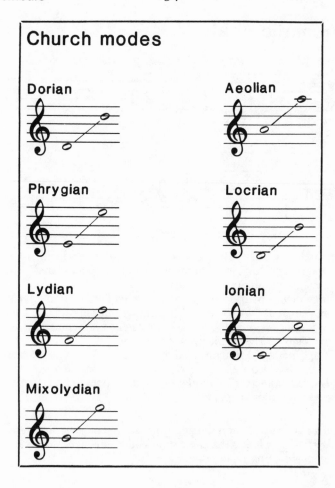

Church modes

Dorian

Aeolian

Phrygian

Locrian

Lydian

Ionian

Mixolydian

See also *enharmonic; key changes;* and **Scales, Keys and Chords.** See illustration, page 35.

claricembalo   (It.) see *harpsichord.*

clarinet   a single-reed instrument that has five sections: mouthpiece, barrel joint, top joint, lower joint, and bell. There are several variations of clarinet, varying in length from 14 inches (clarinet in A flat) to 55 inches (bass clarinet). All except the soprano clarinet in C are transposing instruments, so that actual sound produced is different than the notes as written. The most common

circle of fifths

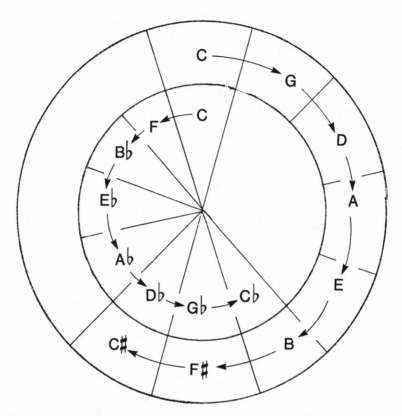

clarinets are in B♭, E♭ and A. See also *transposing instrument; wind family.* See illustration, page 36.

clarinete (Sp.) see *clarinet.*

clarinette (Fr.) see *clarinet.*

clarinetto (It.) see *clarinet.*

classical **(1)** in general, all music except popular music. **(2)** specifically, music composed between 1750 and 1820, preceding the Romantic music period. Classical music is characterized by compositions of Haydn and Mozart. Rules of form and structure were respected and followed, and the concept of including artistic expression and thought in music developed and became acceptable. See also *neoclassicism; pop; Romantic music.*

clavecin (Fr.) see *harpsichord.*

clarinet

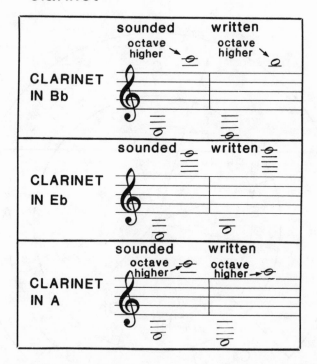

clavecín   (Sp.) see *harpsichord.*

clavichord   the earliest type of keyboard instrument, developed as early as the 12th century. It is constructed of wood and has a three-octave keyboard. Strings are struck from below by prolonged keys. In comparison, a harpsichord's strings are plucked mechanically. The clavichord produces a soft, delicate tone. See also *harpsichord; keyboard instrument; piano.*

clavier   a keyboard, devised from the German word klavier. See also *keyboard; klavier.*

clef   the symbol written at the left of each staff line, to instruct a performer as to pitch and range. See also *alto clef; bass clef; indefinite pitch clef; percussion clef; tenor clef; treble clef;* and **Illustrated Notation Guide.**

clef changes   an instruction on the staff to change from one clef to another. In instruments with ranges that go beyond the convenient range of a single clef, such as piano or cello, staff changes are necessary. See also **Illustrated Notation Guide.** See illustration, page 37.

climax   (1) the height in the development section of a movement, or the moment when conflict in theme or harmony is maximized. (2) a crescendo to the point of maximum volume. See also *crescendo; development; volume.*

clef changes

---

cloches   (Fr.) see *bells.*

close harmony   the placement of voices or parts within as close a range as possible, usually within one octave or less, notably in treble parts. See also *harmony; interval; position; progression.*

---

close harmony

---

cluster   the creation of dissonance by simultaneously sounding several adjacent notes. See also *dissonance; tone cluster.*

---

cluster

---

cocos   (Sp.) see *wood block.*

coda   (It.) the conclusion of a score or movement, added to the end of the main structural sections. In sonata form, the coda section takes place after principal subjects have been recapitulated. See also *recapitulation; sonata form.*

codetta   (It.) the concluding section of an exposition as part of a movement, or a short coda. See also *exposition; movement.*

colla parte   (It.) performance direction to an accompanist, to follow the lead of a soloist in a section set aside for improvisation or free style. See also *accompaniment; improvisation; solo.*

coloratura   (It.) a style of colorful music for soprano voice, designed to show range, vocal quality and virtuosity. See also *soprano; vocal music.*

combination tones   tones that can be heard as the result of loudly playing two other tones. The combination tone's pitch is the difference in frequencies between the two sounded tones. See also *differential tone; resultant tone.*

---

combination tones

---

comic opera   an opera with a comedy plot or light subject matter. See also *opera buffa.*

commodo   (It.) comfortable tempo.

common chord   the first position of a chord, constructed of the interval positions 1, 2 and 3 and sounded in that order. See also *chord; triad.*

---

common chord

major   minor

---

common time   alternative name of 4/4 meter. See also *meter.*

common tone   a tone that occurs in two different chords that are played in sequence. The common tone is held over from one to the other. See also *chord; tone.*

---

common tone

---

compass   the maximum range of an instrument or voice, from lowest to highet note. Some instruments must be described in terms of both maximum compass and chromatic compass, due to the inability to sound certain notes at one end of the range. See also *range.*

complement   descriptive of two successive intervals that, when inverted, represent one full octave. Typical inversion includes the second-seventh, third-sixth, and fourth-fifth. See also *interval; inversion.*

---

complement

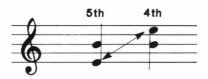

---

composition   the creation of original music through the combination of key, notes, instrumentation, dynamics and harmony; or the arrangement or transcription of an existing piece of music so that its character or texture is changed. See also *arrangement; transcription.*

compound binary form   an expanded version of binary form, in which a theme is introduced, followed by a second theme, and concluding with a repeat of the first theme (A-B-A form). This is also called sonata form. It includes exposition, development and recapitulation of each theme. See also *binary form; first movement form; sonata form.*

compound interval   any interval spanning more than one octave. See also *interval; simple interval.* See illustration, page 40.

compound interval

---

compound meter   a grouping of beats per measure that results when simple meter is multiplied by three. See also *meter; simple meter.*

---

compound meter

simple

compound

---

concert   the public performance of music, involving several musicians or singers and several numbers, or orchestral and voice combinations. See also *choir; ensemble; orchestra.*

concert band   an ensemble of wind, brass and percussion instruments. See also *band; dance band.*

concert pitch   tuning all instruments in an orchestra to the non-transposed A above middle C. See also *note; pitch.*

concertina   an instrument similar to the accordion. However, the concertina employs rows of studs instead of a keyboard to produce the melody. See also *accordion.*

concertino   the smaller grouping of instruments in a concerto grosso; or a small concerto. See also *concerto grosso.*

concertmaster   the orchestra's first violinist. See also *orchestra; violin.*

concerto   a composition for solo instrument and orchestra. Some concertos include two or more solo instruments. The traditional concerto includes three movements in sonata form. The orchestra is one of two sections, and not merely an accompaniment to the solo part. See also *orchestra; solo; sonata form.*

concerto grosso   (It.) "great concert," a four or five movement form popular during the Baroque period, involving two separate instrumental groups, a smaller grouping of soloists and a larger orchestra. See also *Baroque; orchestra.*

concord   a sound that is resolved harmonically, at rest, or fitting in the context of texture; the opposite of discord, an unresovled or unpleasant combination of sound. See also *discord.*

condensed score   a reduced version of a full score, with transposing parts expressed in sounded notes. The condensed score makes it possible to play the composition on a keyboard. See also *orchestration; reduction; score; transcription.*

---

condensed score

---

conduct   to lead and direct the performance of an orchestra or other ensemble. The conductor controls the tempo and dynamics of performance, and coordinates the various sections. This is achieved through hand and body movements, or with the use of a baton. In smaller ensembles, a first violinist, pianist or other leading solist cues other performers with brief movements of the head, hand or instrument. See also *ensemble; orchestra.*

---

conduct

two beats

three beats

four beats

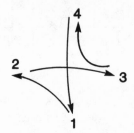

conga **(1)** a Latin dance in 4/4 time, emphasizing the fourth beat of each measure. Performance is usually accompanied with drums and other percussion instruments. **(2)** a tapered, cone-shaped drum that is played from a standing or sitting position. The drum can be held by a sling over the player's shoulders, and is struck with the hands. See also *dance; drum; percussion family; rhythm.*

conjunct notes that occur in sequence above or below one another in the scale. See also *note; scale.*

---

conjunct

---

consecutive interval the movement of two voices or parts in the same direction, so that intervals are repeated in subsequent chords. As a basic rule of theory, consecutive perfect intervals (fourth, fifth and octaves) are highly undesirable. See also *hidden fifth; parallel fifths; similar motion.* See illustration, page 44.

consequent the development of a fugue or other polyphonic composition, in which the subject (antecedent) is followed by the answer (consequent). In the fugue form, the antecedent is written in the tonic key, and the consequent appears in the dominant. See also *antecedent; exposition; fugue; polyphony; real answer; tonal answer.* See illustration, page 45.

console the keyboard, stops and pedals of the organ, those parts that are directly controlled by the performer. See also *keyboard; organ; pedal; stop.*

consonance an agreeable or pleasant sound, within the context of accepted theories of harmony. Intervals of the third are considered consonant, while the second and seventh intervals are dissonant, for example. However, depending on the sequence of chords and the key relationships, what represents consonance or dissonance cannot be easily or consistently determined. See also *dissonance; harmony; interval.*

consort a grouping of instruments, most often applied to chamber ensembles. See also *chamber music; ensemble.*

continuo (It.) a bass accompaniment to music, in which the correct bass notes are sounded in figured bass form. In the Baroque period, composers often wrote coded numbers below the bass line indicating the preferred continuo. Typical continuo direction includes:

consecutive interval

sample arrangement

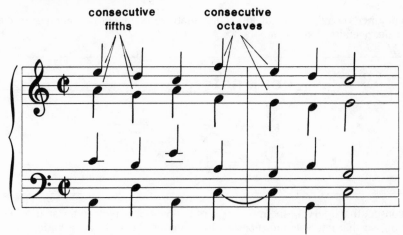

preferred arrangement

sign	continuo
8	root of the triad
6	first inversion of the triad
6/4	second inversion of the triad
7	root of the seventh chord
6/5	first inversion of the seventh chord
4/3	second inversion of the seventh chord
2	third inversion of the seventh chord

consequent

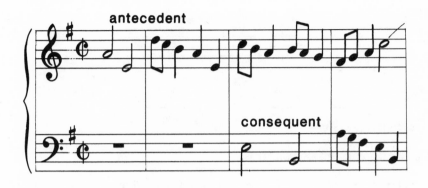

See also *accompaniment; Baroque; figured bass; harmony.*

contrabajo   (Sp.) see *double bass.*

contrabasso   (It.) see *double bass.*

contrabassoon   an orchestral instrument that sounds one full octave below the bassoon. This instrument produces the lowest notes in the orchestra. See also *bassoon; wind family.*

contrabassoon

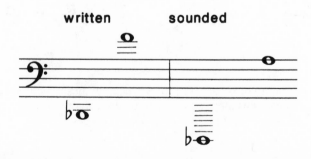

contrabass-tuba   also called the double-bass tuba in B♭ (B-B♭), an instrument that sounds one octave lower than the tenor tuba. It has a total length of 18 feet and is used in military bands. See also *brass family; tuba.* See illustration, page 46.

contra-bass tuba

contrafagote   (Sp.) see *contrabassoon*.

contrafagotto   (It.) see *contrabassoon*.

contralto   the third highest voice, below soprano and mezzo soprano, more often abbreviated as alto. See also *alto*.

contrapuntal   descriptive of music written in counterpoint form, meaning "note against note." This is the utilization of two or more themes sounding at the same time. See also *counterpoint; polyphony*.

contrary motion   the movement of two themes or melodies in opposite directions. See also *motion; polyphony*.

contrary motion

contratenor   (It.) a voice part used in 15th century music, written below the tenor range. Today, this range is assigned to alto, baritone or bass voices. See also *alto; baritone; bass; tenor; vocal music*.

contrebasse   (Fr.) see *double bass*.

contrebasson   (Fr.) see *contrabassoon*.

convertible counterpoint   the reversal of contrapuntal parts, from high to low voice or from low to high voice. See also *invertible counterpoint*.

coperto   (It.) covered (muted percussion).

cor Anglais   (Fr.) see *English horn.*

cor de basset   (Fr.) see *basset horn.*

cor d'harmonie   (Fr.) see *valve horn.*

corda   (It.) open string.

cornamusa   (It.) see *bagpipe.*

cornemuse   (Fr.) see *bagpipe.*

cornet   a three-valve brass instrument in B flat, less often used in orchestral scores than the valve trumpet. See also *brass family; trumpet.*

---

cornet

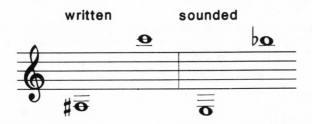

---

corneta   (Sp.) see *cornet.*

cornetta   (It.) see *cornet.*

corno   (It.) (Sp.) see *valve horn.*

corno de basset   (Fr.) see *basset horn.*

corno di bassetto   (Sp.) see *basset horn.*

corno Ingles   (Sp.) see *English horn.*

corno Inglese   (It.) see *English horn.*

counter fugue   a fugue in which the consequent is written as an inversion of the antecedent. See also *antecedent; cancrizans; consequent; fugue; inversion; mirror fugue.* See illustration, page 48.

counter fugue

---

countermelody a melody of secondary importance to the primary melody or theme, similar to the common, although inaccurate meaning assigned to obbligato. See also *melody; obbligato; theme.*

counterpoint a composition with two or more melodies, each of equal importance, but with offsetting or competing range and tone. The effect is to add texture in polyphonic form. In addition to harmonic variations, offsetting rhythms advance the total effect. See also *melody; polyphony; texture.*

---

counterpoint

---

countersubject a secondary theme found is some fugues that appears in counterpoint to the main theme. See also *melody; theme.*

countertenor   an exceptionally high male voice, above normal tenor range and closer to alto. See also *alto; range; tenor; voice.*

coupler   a device on an organ enabling the performer to transfer stops and other features available on one keyboard, to another; or to couple a keyboard with the pedals. See also *keyboard; organ; pedal; stop.*

courante   a French dance developed before the 17th century, and later evolved as a standard section in the suite. The courante is written in 6/4 or 3/2 time, with frequent shifts in emphasis and rhythm, giving the dance a contrapuntal quality. See also *counterpoint; dance; suite.*

crécelle   (Fr.) see *rattle.*

crescendo   (It.) increasing in volume. See also *decrescendo; dynamic mark; fork; volume.*

---

crescendo

---

crook   a device on some brass instruments that can be removed to change keys. With the modern use of valves, the crook is not used today to the same degree as before the 19th century. See also *brass family.*

cross fingering   method of performing on a wind or keyboard instrument, in which fingering is done in other than the usual sequence. See also *fingering; keyboard instrument; wind family.*

cross hand   in keyboard playing, the crossing of one hand over the other. Performance directions for cross hand are written as r.h. (right hand) or l.h. (left hand). See also *fingering; keyboard instrument.*

cross relation   the occurrence of two notes in successive chords that are a half step apart, but appearing in different voices or parts. The preferred method is to write the two chords with cross related notes in the same part. See also *false relations; half step.* See illustration, page 50.

cross rhythm   the use of two unlike rhythms at the same time, either by combining meter notation, or altering one part. For example, in 4/4 time, cross rhythm is achieved by writing the bass part in triplets. See also *polyrhythm; rhythm.* See illustration, page 50.

cross relation

cross rhythm

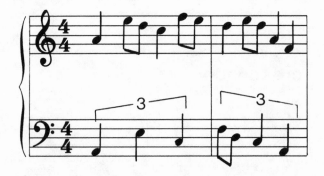

crossbeam   the line connecting groupings of notes of less value than a quarter note. See also *beam*.

crossbeam

crotchet   see *quarter note*.

crush note   a grace note played on a keyboard instrument at the same moment as the subject note, and immediately released. See also *grace note*.

cue   a method of giving a signal to a performer after a long rest in the score. It oftens involves reproducing a reduced version of another instrument's part. See also *orchestration; rest*. See illustration, page 51.

cue

---

cycle **(1)** a group of songs or movements played in sequence, as in a suite. **(2)** a term sometimes used to describe the ascending and descending fifth in key relationships, more commonly called the circle of fifths. See also *circle of fifths; song; suite.*

cyclical symphony a symphony in which themes or recognizable attributes of themes are repeated or imitated in more than one movement. See also *movement; symphony; theme.*

cymbal (alt. cymbals) an indefinite pitch instrument consisting of two circular brass plates and a hand strap. They can be played in several ways. In orchestral use, they are clashed together or struck with a drumstick. In bands they are mounted on a stand and struck with drumsticks or a wire brush. See also *percussion family.*

cymbale (Fr.) see *cymbal.*

D

da capo (D.C.) (It.) repeat from the beginning.

da capo aria an aria in ABA form. It contains three sections, with the third a repeat of the first. See also *aria; opera.*

dal segno (D.S.) (It.) repeat from the sign.

damper part of a piano's mechanism that stops the strings from vibrating after release of the key. It is a rectangular section of wood covered with felt, located directly above each string. To offset the effect, the sustain pedal lifts the damper and allows strings to continue vibrating. See also *keyboard instrument; piano; sustain pedal.*

dance regulated or planned physical movement to the accompaniment of music, originally ritualistic or performed in honor of deities or as forms of artistic expression. Forms originally designed strictly as dances have been incorporated into instrumental compositions, as sections of suites, symphonies and other forms. See also *ballet; modern dance.*

dance band an instrumental group that performs jazz or popular music, made up of brass, woodwind and percussion instruments. See also *band; jazz; pop.*

dance poem a serious orchestral work intended for interpretation through dance. See also *ballet; choreographic poem; symphonic poem.*

dead interval the relationship between two notes or chords, when phrases are separated by a rest. See also *interval; phrase; rest.*

dead interval

decay the gradual reduction of sound. In music, a fade is used as a transition from one mood to another or to end a movement. See also *diminuendo; dynamic mark; volume.*

deceptive cadence a cadence in which the sounding of one chord anticipates the chord to follow, but another chord is substituted. For example, the dominant chord is followed not by the tonic, but by a sixth. See also *cadence; chord; interval; progression.* See illustration, page 53.

decibel the standard measurement of sound, or one-tenth of a bel. See also *bel; volume.*

decrescendo (It.) decreasing in volume. See also *crescendo; dynamic mark; fork; volume.* See illustration, page 53.

degree the position of a note in the scale, assigned names or numbers; or, in solmization an abbreviated name:

degree	name	solmization
1	tonic	doh
2	supertonic	ray
3	mediant	me
4	subdominant	fah

deceptive cadence

I   IV   V   VI

decrescendo

degree (con't.)

5	dominant	soh
6	submediant	lah
7	leading tone	te

See also *dominant; interval; leading tone; mediant; scale; solmization; subdominant; submediant; super-tonic; tonic.*

degree

1ST 2ND 3RD 4TH 5TH 6TH 7TH

delicato   (It.) delicately.

demisemiquaver   the English term for a thirty-second note. See also *thirty-second note.*

descant   the highest voice or part, often used to describe an obbligato section in music. See also *obbligato; soprano.*

development   the expansion, modification, and elaboration on a theme, as found in sonata form. It occurs after the exposition. Composition techniques of development include modulaton, changes from major to minor keys, extensions of rhythm, mingling of themes in contrapuntal form, inversion, fragmentation or extension, and changes to the theme. The possible techniques and combinations of development are unlimited. See also *exposition; motive; recapitulation; sonata form; theme.*

diapason   the control over tone and volume on an organ. The diapason can be set to open (louder) or stopped (softer) positions. See also *organ; stopped.*

diatonic   the major and minor scales in popular use in western music. The diatonic major scale has a half step between the third and fourth degrees, and between the seventh and eighth degrees; all other degrees are separated by whole notes. The minor diatonic scale is constructed in one of three ways, by modifying the major scale:
    harmonic minor—reduction by one half step of the third and sixth degrees.
    melodic minor—reduction by one half step of the third degree.
    natural minor—reduction by one half step of the third, sixth and seventh degrees.
    See also *chromatic scale; harmonic minor scale; interval; major scale; melodic minor scale; minor scale; natural minor scale; scale; and* **Scales, Keys and Chords.** See illustration, page 55.

dieses   (It.) sharp.

dièze   (Fr.) sharp.

differential tone   a third tone heard when two other tones are sounded loudly. Its frequency value is the difference in frequencies between the other two tones. See also *combination tones; resultant tone.* See illustration, page 55.

diminished chord   a chord with the third and fifth degrees lowered by one half step. See also *chord; interval.* See illustration, page 56.

diminuendo   (It.) gradually softer.

diminution   the reduction of note value, often used in the fugue, or as part of the development of a theme. See also *augmentation; counterpoint; development; fugue.* See illustration, page 56.

dinuovo   (It.) once again.

diatonic

Major

Harmonic Minor

Melodic Minor

Natural Minor

differential tone

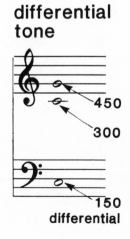

differential

diminished chord

diminution

original theme

diminution

dirge   music written for performance during a funeral. See also *lament.*

discant   descriptive of vocal or instrumental music with single melodies supported by chords; or polyphonic elaborations of metrically offsetting melodies over a lower, sustained bass. See also *homophonic sound; polyphony; song.*

discord   an unresolved or unpleasant sound produced by a chord. See also *chord; concord; resolution.*

dissonance   an effect created by the sounding of certain chords and intervals. Dissonance has been defined as an unpleasant sound. However, what constitutes dissonance has changed over time. In addition, the placement of chords in the context of music may create unpleasant effects, even when those chords are consonant. Examples of this effect include close harmony in lower ranges, assigning notes to extremely high ranges of instruments, and the introduction of a consonant chord in a different key. See also *chord; consonance; interval.*

divertimento   (It.) a diversion, a composition with between four and ten short movements for one instrument or a small ensemble. Some of these pieces are combinations of the sonata form and variations of other forms. See also *sonata form; suite.*

divisi   (It.) a section of music divided into two parts. See also *instrumentation.*

divisions   an outdated term meaning variations, derived from the practice of splitting note time values into smaller units. See also *variation.*

dodecaphonic   12-tone music. See also *twelve-tone music.*

dodecuple sound   the chromatic scale, in which each note is of equal value, as applied to 12-tone music. See also *chromatic scale; twelve-tone music.*

doh   the first degree of the scale, in the solmization system. See also *degree; solmization; tonic.*

dolce   (It.) sweetly and softly.

dolcissimo   (It.) very softly.

dolente   (It.) sadly.

doloroso   (It.) sorrowfully.

dominant   the fifth degree of the scale, a perfect interval with the tonic and an inversion of the perfect fourth. See also *interval; perfect interval; tonic.*

---

dominant

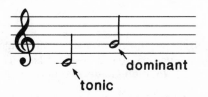

doppio movimento   (It.) double speed.

Dorian mode   a Church mode beginning and ending on the note D, utilizing only the natural tones in between. See also *Church modes; mode.* See illustration, page 58.

dot   a period used in notation for staccato (placed above the note) or to extend time value by half (placed after the note). See also **Illustrated Notation Guide.** See illustration, page 58.

Dorian mode

dot

dotted note a note whose time value has been extended by half. This technique avoids using a greater number of smaller notes. Two dots after a note indicate time value is cut by half, and then by half again. See also *rhythm;* and **Illustrated Notation Guide.**

dotted note

double bar two vertical lines drawn through a staff to signal a change in key or meter, a repeat, or the end of a piece. See also *key signature; repeat; time signature;* and **Illustrated Notation Guide.** See illustration, page 59.

double bass the largest instrument in the string family, with the lowest range. It is also called the bass viol. Open strings are tuned to E, A, D and G, and on some instruments, a fifth string extends the range downward to open string C. It sounds one octave lower than as written. See also *bass viol; string family.* See illustration, page 59.

double concerto a concerto that employs two separate solo instruments and an orchestra, so that the composition has three separate sections. See also *concerto.*

double counterpoint descriptive of counterpoint in which the lower part, if

double bar

key change

time change

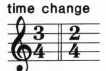

repeats

end

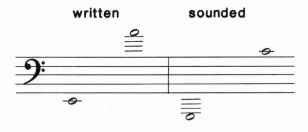

double bass

written   **sounded**

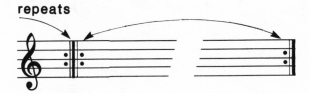

raised an octave, becomes the higher part, while the original high part is inverted to the bass. See also *counterpoint; invertible counterpoint.* See illustration, page 60.

double counterpoint

original theme

inverted theme

---

double flat   notation to lower a note's pitch by two half tones. This is made necessary in certain keys, where the note to be diminished is already a flat. However, on most instruments, the result of the double flat is to sound the note one full step below. See also *accidental; flat*.

---

double flat

---

double fugue   a fugue involving two separate themes, one following the other or both performed simultaneously. See also *fugue; quadruple fugue; triple fugue*. See illustration, page 61.

double pedal   technique in organ music, calling for the use of both feet to play separate sections on the pedals. See also *organ; pedal*.

double quartet   (1) a composition for two separate quartets of instruments. In this form, the two quartets are distinct from one another in form and relationship. In an octet, however, each of the eight instruments acts as an independent

double fugue

first theme

second theme

---

part. **(2)** a vocal quartet in which each of four parts is doubled by two singers. See also *octet; quartet; string quartet; vocal music.*

double reed   a set of two reeds used on certain woodwind instruments, such as the oboe. See also *oboe; reed; wind family.*

double sharp   notation to raise a pitch by two half tones, made necessary in keys where the tone to be augmented is already a sharp. On most instruments, the result is to sound the note one full step above. See also *accidental; sharp.*

---

double sharp

---

double sonata-allegro form   a variation on the sonata-allegro form used in some concertos. Rather than repeating the exposition section in exact form, it is written out twice. The solo instrument is not introduced until the second version. As the second theme in the exposition is repeated, there is a modulation to another key, usually the dominant. See also *concerto; exposition; form; sonata-allegro form.*

double stop   the playing of two strings or more at the same time, in string music. See also *due corde; string family.*

double-tongue   articulation of notes in woodwind and brass instruments. The notation is written out only in instructional music. See also *brass family; tonguing; triple-tongue; wind family.*

double–tongue

double trio   **(1)** a composition containing a repeated middle secton in ABABA form. **(2)** a vocal composition in which three separate parts are each sung by two performers. See also *string trio; trio; vocal music.*

double triplet   a sextuplet divided into two groups of three notes each, rather than the more usual division consisting of three groups of two notes each. See also *irregular grouping; sextuplet.*

double triplet

douleur   (Fr.) sadly.

down beat   the first beat of a measure, or the movement of a conductor's hand or baton (downward) at the first beat of each measure. See also *beat; conduct; measure; up beat.*

down-bow   a method of playing a stringed instrument, by pulling the bow toward the performer. The opposite, an up-beat, involves pushing the bow away from the performer. Notation for the down-bow is a squared, inverted U. See also *string family; up-bow.* See illustration, page 63.

down-bow

---

drone **(1)** a sustained bass note. **(2)** the bass accompaniment tone of the bagpipe. See also *bagpipe.*

drum a percussion instrument made of stretched skin or membrane, over a hollow space. Drums are played by being struck with a stick or brush, or by the hand. The tympani is the only orchestral drum with definite pitch. Other drums' parts are written on the percussion, or indefinite pitch clef. These include the snare, tenor and bass drums, and the tambourine. See also *bass drum; indefinite pitch clef; kettledrum; percussion family; snare drum; tambourine; tenor drum; tympani.*

dudelsack (G.) see *bagpipe.*

due corde (It.) **(1)** played on two strings, an instruction in string music involving one open string and another that is depressed. **(2)** instruction in piano music to use the soft pedal, which reduces the number of strings struck when notes are played. See also *piano; string family.*

duet a song for two voices, or an instrumental composition for two instruments. See also *instrumentation; song; vocal music.*

dulcimer a string instrument employing hammers to strike strings, as in the action of a piano but in a more compacted space. The instrument is similar to the psaltery and the zither, both of which are plucked rather than struck. See also *piano; psaltery; zither.*

dumka an Eastern European folk song characterized by swift tempo and mood changes. See also *folk music; song.*

duple meter meter involving two beats per measure. See also *meter.* See illustration, page 64.

duplet a grouping of two beats where the meter is for three, similar to the triplet (three beats in place of two). See also *irregular grouping; meter; triplet.* See illustration, page 64.

dur (G.) major key.

dynamic mark notation for the degrees of volume to be used in performance of music, including:

duple meter

duplet

mark	Italian	English
ppp	pianississimo	extremely soft
pp	pianissimo	very soft
p	piano	soft
mp	mezzo piano	moderately soft
mf	mezzo forte	moderately loud
f	forte	loud
ff	fortissimo	very loud
fff	fortississimo	extremely loud

See also *volume*.

dynamism   a style of music including strong dissonance and rhythm, irregular meter, and colorful arrangements, popularized in early 20th century compositions by Stravinsky. See also *dissonance; orchestration; rhythm.*

E

ear training   the study of music, for the purpose of developing and improving comprehension. Ear trained students learn to identify pitch, intervals, rhythm and harmony. Also studied are part writing, harmonization, and sight reading.

Relative pitch, the recognition of pitch by relation to range and tone quality, is an important part of ear training. The ability to hear and identify intrinsic qualities of music, or visualizing what one hears, can be taught, although professionals naturally develop ear training through exposure and practice. See also *harmony; relative pitch; sight read; tonal imagery.*

échappée   a rhythmically weak nonharmonic tone identified by the motion of the tone, which is opposite of, or away from the resolution note. See also *harmony; nonharmonic tone; rhythm.*

échappée

eighth note   a note with one-half the value of a quarter note, indicated by a single flag or, when two or more appear together, by a single bar. In 6/8 time, there are six eight notes per bar. In 4/4 time, the maximum number of eighth notes is eight (four quarter notes or, if valued are halved, eight eighth notes. See also *notation; quaver;* and **Illustrated Notation Guide.**

eighth note

eighth rest

eighth rest   a rest—pause in sound—with a time value equal to one-half that of a quarter rest. For example, in 6/8 time, each bar will contain combinations of notes and rests equalling six counts of eighth notes or rests. See also *rest;* and **Illustrated Notation Guide.** See illustration, page 65.

eilend (G.) hurridly.

élan (Fr.) with dash.

electronic instrument any instrument whose sound is enhanced or produced by electronic means. Electronic sound production is a relatively new advancement in music, and represents a departure from the traditional methods of creating music, by plucking, striking, or sounding with the lips. See also *steel guitar; synthesizer.*

electronic music music composed specifically for performance on electronic instruments or ensembles. Some forms of electronic music are created directly by the composer, without the involvement or interpretation of a performer. For example, music can be created and sounded on a home computer. In this instance, the composer can cause the composing medium to also perform music. See also *composition.*

elegy a sad, poetic composition. See also *lament.*

elevation a short composition for the organ, played as part of the Catholic church service (during the elevation of the host). See also *organ.*

eleventh a compound interval (one exceeding an octave) of 11 diatonic steps, or one octave plus a fourth. See also *compound interval; interval.*

---

eleventh

---

embellishment a device that adds flavor to music, through alteration of rhythm, addition of ornaments, trills, mordents, or turns. See also *ornament;* and **Illustrated Notation Guide.**

embouchure (alt. embrochure) the positioning of a performer's lips in playing brass or wind instruments. See also *brass family; wind family.*

energico (It.) energetically.

Englischhorn (G.) see *English horn.*

English flute   an outdated name for the recorder. See also *recorder*.

English horn   an instrument in the oboe family, played with a double reed mouthpiece. It sounds in the alto range and is pitched a fifth below the oboe's range. See also *oboe; transposing instrument; wind family*.

English horn

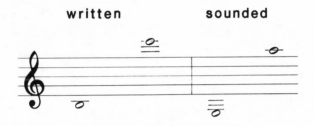

enharmonic   notes that are written differently but are sounded identically. For example, an F flat is the same sound as an E natural on the piano, and a C sharp is the same tone as a D flat. In theory, these tones have different values in unlike keys, and some instruments—notably in the string family—can be played with subtle differences in tone, depending on the key. Enharmonics can apply to intervals and chords as well as to single notes. See also *chord; interval*.

enharmonic

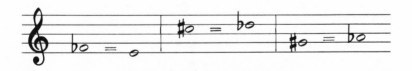

ensemble   **(1)** a group of performers, either vocal or instrumental; or both. **(2)** term used is describing the quality or balance of a performance. See also *choir; orchestra*.

entry   the start of a theme during a fugue, or the point where a voice begins (enters). For example, the first instrument introduces the theme in measure one; and the second instrument enters in the second measure. See also *fugue*. See illustration, page 68.

entry

episode (1) in a fugue, rondo or other form, a section of music not related to the primary theme, or that serves only to connect two sections of thematic material. (2) a composition or part of a larger composition containing loosely constructed, unrelated sections, such as a suite containing unlike material or styles. See also *fugue; rondo form; suite.*

equal marks

equal marks notation used to indicate the meaning or relationship of time or tempo. For example, when time signature changes from 3/4 to 4/4, a notation is made above the staff, showing the previous and new values of notes per measure. Example: the composer describes the tempo as "allegro." To be more specific, a quarter note is written above, followed by equal marks and the number 176. This means that there should be 176 counts per minute. See also *notation; tempo; time signature.* See illustration, page 68.

equal temperament   the method of tuning instruments, based on the division of an octave into twelve equal parts. Each tone in the octave in tuned equally, one half tone apart. See also *interval; just intonation; temperament; unequal temperament.*

equal voices   descriptive of vocal music written exclusively for all male or for all female voices, but not for both. See also *range; vocal music.*

espressione   (It.) expressively.

etude   (Fr.) a composition designed to help students master an instrument, or to practice a technique. See also *composition; exercise; finger exercise.*

eufonio   (It.) (Sp.) see *euphonium.*

euphonium   a brass instrument used in bands, with a fourth valve enabling players to extend its range. See also *band; brass family; horn.*

exercise   **(1)** a short composition for piano. **(2)** a piece for voice or an instrument, designed for practice value rather than artistic expression. Its purpose is to help students improve technique and skill. See also *etude; finger exercise; piano; vocal music.*

exposition   the section in sonata form or in a fugue, in which a theme is first introduced. See also *development; fugue; sonata form; theme.*

expressif   (Fr.) expressively.

expression   the technique, creative performance or interpretation of music. Composers may indicate the desired mood of a piece through notation. However, performers may bring their own interpretation to the actual performance. See also *composition.*

expressionism   a musical trend developed in response to impressionism, beginning in the 1920s. This concept attempts to demonstrate the composer's or performer's state of mind through the musical statement. While impressionism as characterized by compositions of Debussy emphasized liquidity in style and form, expressionism is the opposite. It is more graphic, morbid, harsh, and dissonant. The idea of expressionism derives from popular trends of the time, seen in art and drama. See also *impressionism.*

extemporization   free style, improvisational or spontaneous performance of music as popularized in jazz. In comparison, traditional forms of music are highly structured, with precise meter, volume, and notes indicated in full. See also *improvisation; jazz.*

extended rest   a period of silence lasting two or more full measures. In orchestral music, extended rests are common, as many instruments play only in specific parts of a particular composition. This rest is summarized with a lengthened rest symbol, and the number of rests are written above the staff. See also *rest;* and **Illustrated Notation Guide.**

---

extended rest

F

facilement   (Fr.) easily.

facilmente   (It.) easily.

fagote   (Sp.) see *bassoon.*

fagott   (G.) see *bassoon.*

fagotto   (It.) see *bassoon.*

fah   the fourth degree of the diatonic scale, also called the subdominant. See also *degree; solmization; subdominant.*

false cadence   see *deceptive cadence.*

false fingering   a method of playing an instrument other than in the standard or accepted method. This is appropriate when the normal fingering method is difficult or awkward, when a special effect is being created, or when sequences before or after a section make exceptions necessary. See also *fingering.*

false octave   a technique used in piano scores in which a rapid series of alternating octaves and single notes are played, to create the effect of progressive octaves. See also *octave; piano.* See illustration, page 71.

false relation   see *cross relation.*

false triad   an outdated term meaning the same as the diminished fifth. See also *diminished chord; fifth; triad.*

false octave

played

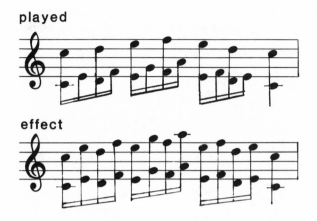

effect

---

falsetto   (It.) an artifical method of singing with which a tenor is able to reach notes above his range. See also *alto; tenor; vocal music.*

familiar style   a style of vocal music in which note values are equal and all voices sing the same text at the same time. This is a common style in church hymns. See also *block chords; hymn; vocal music.*

---

familiar style

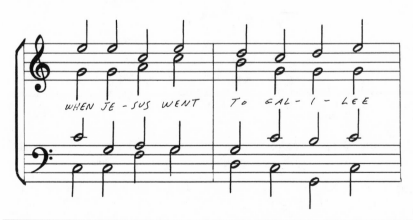

WHEN JE - SUS WENT   TO GAL - I - LEE

---

family   a grouping of instruments by section, based on similarities in tone quality of performance method. In the orchestra, there are four major families:

strings, winds, brass and percussion. See also *brass family; percussion family; string family; wind family.*

fancy   a form of 16th century music for strings, written in contrapuntal style and employing rapid tempo and meter changes. See also *contrapuntal.*

fandango   a Spanish dance in 3/4 time, characterized by two-measure rhythms emphasizing the first and last beats of the first measure and the second beat of the second measure. The fandango is often accompanied by guitar and castanets. See also *dance; rhythm.*

fandango

fanfare   a ceremonial introduction or musical announcement, often as short as two measures. It is played on a brass instrument in tones of the triad. See also *brass family; flourish; horn.*

fanfare

fantasy   **(1)** a modern name for the 16th and 17th century fancy. **(2)** a style of composition that does not follow the traditional rules of form. **(3)** a term sometimes applied to short pieces or to variations of themes. See also *fancy; form; style; theme and variations.*

farandole   a dance of French origin, written in 3/4 or 6/8 time, performed by a chain of people following the motions of a leader. See also *dance.*

farce   a musical or dramatic production of a comical, satirical and sometimes risque nature, or music that imitates other styles. See also *comic opera; opera.*

fasola   a method of identifying the degrees of the scale, by assigning one-syllable names to each. The system was used in England and the United States

fasola

doh ray mi fah soh lah ti

---

in the 17th and 18th centuries, and employed only four tones: fa, so, la and mi.

The system originated in the 11th century to help singers identify the correct notes of the hexachord in vocal scores. The names for each note come from Latin words beginning each of six phrases in a Gregorian chant, the *Hymn to St. John the Baptist,* also called *Ut Queant Laxis.* The original fasola names were assigned by a Benedictine monk named Guido d'Arezzo (c. 995–1050).

The six phrases began on each of the six tones in the hexachord. The seventh degree was not part of this original system, but was added later, when the modern diatonic scale was developed:

degree	fasola name	original name	modern name
1	fa	ut	doh (do)
2	sol	re	ray (re)
3	la	mi	mi
4	fa	fa	fah (fa)
5	sol	sol	soh (so, sol)
6	la	la	lah (la)
7	mi		ti (te)

The seventh degree, when first added to the fasola system, was called si, and was later changed to ti or, sometimes, te.

It must be remembered that the names assigned to the degrees are somewhat arbitrary. Their only purpose is to distinguish one degree from another, and different names are used in systems in various countries and even regions. It is useful for identifying degrees of the scale regardless of the key in use.

The fasola system has been expanded to a chromatic variation, with assigned names for all degrees of the scale:

degree	ascending name	degree	descending name
1	do	7	ti
1 sharp	di	7 flat	te
2	re	6	la
2 sharp	ri	6 flat	le
3	mi	5	sol
4	fa	5 flat	se
4 sharp	fi	4	fa

5	sol	3	mi
5 sharp	si	3 flat	me
6	la	2	re
6 sharp	li	2 flat	ra
7	ti	1	do

See also *degree; hexachord; solmization.*

faux bourdon   (Fr.) false bass, the harmonization of a Gregorian chant in the following manner: Every chord is written in the first inversion (from bottom to top, the mediant, dominant and tonic), while phrases begin and end with open fifth chords (tonic, dominant, tonic). Although primitive, the faux bourdon is an early example (14th and 15th century) of the use of triads in harmony, and is part of the early development of modern harmonic practice. See also *dominant; Gregorian chant; harmony; root; third; tonic; triad.*

faux bourdon

feminine cadence   a final cadence that occurs on a measure's weak beat. In comparison, a masculine cadence is one that ends on a strong beat. See also *cadence; masculine cadence.*

feminine cadence

feminine theme   a secondary theme in the sonata or sonata-allegro form. Of the two themes, the stronger is referred to as masculine, while the more passive or reserved theme is called feminine. See also *masculine theme; sonata-allegro form; theme.*

fermata   (It.) the holding of a note, chord or rest beyond its usual time value. The precise amount of time is left to the discretion of the performer or, in ensembles, of the conductor. If placed over a rest, the length of the pause is extended. And if placed over a bar line, there is a pause between measures where one would not normally occur. See also *pause* and **Illustrated Notation Guide.**

fermata

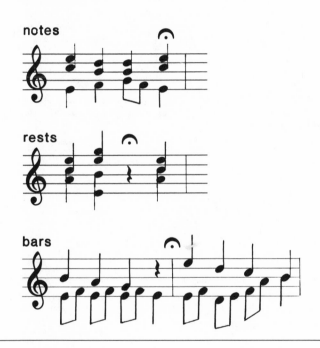

notes

rests

bars

feroce   (It.) ferociously.

fervore   (It.) with fervor.

festivo   (It.) festively.

fiato   (It.) breath (wind instrument notation).

fiddle   **(1)** slang name for the violin, or for any of the smaller stringed instruments played with a bow. **(2)** the violin, when played in the style of folk music. See also *folk music; string family; violin.*

fife a wooden flute of high range without keys, or a transverse flute with up to eight finger holes and a number of keys. See also *flute; wind family.*

fifre (Fr.) see *fife.*

fifteenth a compound interval equal to two octaves. See also *compound interval; interval; octave.*

fifteenth

fifth a perfect interval of five diatonic steps, such as the space between the tonic and the dominant, or the fifth degree of the scale. See also *degree; interval; perfect interval.*

fifth

figure the arrangement of a series of tones in a recognizable pattern. Recognition comes from distinctive harmonic qualities or, more often, from the repetitive nature of the figure, usually in the bass. See also *accompaniment; Alberti bass.* See illustration, page 77.

figured bass a keyboard composition method developed in the Baroque period, combining improvised chords in the right hand, over a bass note and coded numerals beneath. The figured numerals tell the player what chords and inversions are to be played in the treble section.

In keyboard music of the Baroque period, full parts were not written out. Rather, the keyboard player used the figured bass to construct chords or approximations, with some lattitude allowed. This abbreviated form of notation did not dictate the melody line, only the accompaniment to other instruments. In the opinion of composers of the day, the important parts of music were the top and bottom voices, and the middle could be filled in by the performer. An exception to this is found in highly structured or contrapuntal compositions. See also *Baroque; basso continuo; continuo; thorough bass.*

figure

---

final **(1)** in English usage, the tonic note of a key. **(2)** in French usage, a finale. See also *tonic*.

finale **(1)** the last ensemble portion in an act of an opera, or the final act of the opera. **(2)** the final movement of an orchestral work. **(3)** the last portion of a composition's last movement. See also *ensemble; movement; opera*.

fine (It.) the end.

finger board the section of a stringed instrument on which the player's fingers depress strings to change length, thus alter actual notes sounded. See also *string family*.

finger exercise a passage written for practice by keyboard instrument students. The intention is to improve dexterity and finger strength. See also *exercise; keyboard instrument*.

---

finger exercise

---

finger holes holes in the body of a wind instrument that, when covered, alter sound. Previously activated by the fingers directly, these holes are now operated by keys on most modern orchestral instruments. See also *wind family*.

fingering the method and sequence of placing fingers during performance. In piano scores, notably for students, preferred fingering often is indicated in the part. See also *piano; position.*

fingering

1 2 3 1 2 3 4 5 5 4 3 2 1 3 2 1

fipple   a piece of wood that forces air into a canal, to produce sound in certain blown instruments, such as the recorder. See also *recorder; wind family.*

first   **(1)** the tonic, or first degree of the scale. **(2)** the leading performer in a divided section of instruments, playing the higher of two parts (such as the first violin versus second violin). **(3)** the leader of a section, such as first chair in a violin section. See also *degree; tonic.*

first

first inversion   the position of a chord when the triad is arranged with the mediant in the lowest (bass) position. See also *chord; inversion; mediant; root; triad.* See illustration, page 79.

first movement form   see *sonata form.*

fischietto   (It.) see *whistle.*

five-part form   an expansion of the ABA form of music, or ternary form. Five-part form includes mutliple themes, repeated in a series. With two themes, five-part has the sequence ABABA. With three separate themes, the form is ABACA. See also *form; ternary form.*

five-three chord   the position of a chord when the fifth and third are written above the root, also called the root chord. In figured bass, this position is indicated by the notation of 5 over 3 below the bass line. See also *figured bass; root.* See illustration, page 79.

first inversion

five–three chord

flageolet   an obsolete six-holed instrument similar to the recorder. See also *recorder; wind family.*

flageolet tones   the harmonic sounds created on stringed instruments by lightly touching, rather than depressing strings. See also *harmonics; string family.*

flageolett   (G.) see *flageolet.*

flam   a two-note stroke on a snare drum. See also *percussion family; snare drum.*

flat   a note lowered by one half step. See also *accidental; half step; sharp.* See illustration, page 80.

flauta   (Sp.) see *flute.*

flat

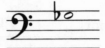

---

flautato (It.) (alt. flautando) **(1)** direction in string music to bow lightly near the finger board, producing a delicate, or flute-like tone. **(2)** sometimes used in string music to indicate the producing of harmonics. See also *finger board; harmonics; string family.*

flaute de pico (Sp.) see *recorder.*

flautín (Sp.) see *fife.*

flautino (It.) see *flageolet.*

flauto (It.) see *flute.*

flauto a becco (It.) see *recorder.*

flauto piccolo (It.) see *piccolo.*

flebile (It.) mournfully.

flehend (G.) imploringly.

flicorno (It.) see *bugle.*

flisocorno (Sp.) See *bugle.*

florid term describing highly ornamental music, notably in operas written in the 18th century. See also *opera; ornament.*

flöte (Gr.) see *flute.*

flourish see *fanfare.*

flute a non-transposing wind instrument with a three-octave range beginning at middle C. Although classified as woodwind, the flute is constructed entirely of metal. It is cross-blown as opposed to vertically-blown instruments such as the recorder, or reed-blown instruments such as the oboe, clarinet and bassoon. The flute has a brilliant tone in its middle range. See also *piccolo; wind family.* See illustration, page 81.

flûte (Fr.) see *flute.*

flute

---

flûte à bec   (Fr.) see *recorder.*

flûte à coulisse   (Fr.) see *slide whistle.*

folk music   songs that derive from regions or nations, and have traits unique to the character of the people, often of a nationalistic tone. Folk music is usually based on legends and folk lore of the country. See also *ballad; nationalism.*

foot   the range of notes an instrument can play, as measured by the length of its pipes or tubes. An organ's pipes are described by length, with lower pitches having greater size. Brass and wind instrument ranges are also dependent on the length of the tubes. See also *brass family; organ; wind family.*

fork   slang term used to describe the notation for increases and decreases in volume. See also *crescendo; decrescendo.*

---

fork

crescendo   decrescendo

---

form   the structure and organization of music into controlled and predictable sound, pitch, harmony, texture and rhythm. Every composition follows one form or another, even beyond this basic definition. At various periods in music history, a form of one name has taken on expanded or even completely different meaning. Thus, a complete definition of form must be further defined in the context of the period involved. In modern application, exceptions to the rule are common. However, this does not mean that rules of harmony and rhythm are suspended, only that form itself is continuously evolving.

Forms are singular or composite. Singular forms include:
—*strophic,* or the use of a single theme.

—*variations* on a single theme.
—*binary* form, or two themes in one work.
—*ternary* form, also known as ABA.
—*sonata* form.
—*four-part,* or ABAC form.
—*five-part,* or ABABA form.
—*rondo,* or ABACABA form.
—*through-composed* forms, or material that is not repeated in the work.
—*imitative* form, including the fugue, motet and use of polyphonic texture.
Composite forms include instrumental music, such as the concerto, symphony, sonata, suite, and other ensemble works; and vocal music, such as the cantata and opera. See also *binary form; five-part form; four-part form; orchestration; rondo form; sonata form; strophic form; ternary form; variation; vocal music.*

forte (f) (It.) loud.

forte-piano (fp) (It.) loud, then soft.

fortissimo (ff) (It.) very loud.

fortississimo (fff) (It.) extremely loud.

forzando (fz) (It.) with force.

fouet (Fr.) see *whip.*

four-part form a form of music in which three separate themes are performed, in the sequence of ABAC. See also *form; sonata form.*

fourth a perfect interval of four diatonic steps, such as the space between the tonic and the subdominant, or the fourth degree of the scale. See also *degree; interval; perfect interval.*

---

fourth

---

fourth chord a chord consisting of a series of fourth intervals, sometimes used by composers in place of the more traditional series of intervals of the third. See also *chord; interval.* See illustration, page 83.

freddo (It.) coldly.

fourth chord

French horn   the horn in F, referred to simply as the horn in all countries except the United States, where "French" is added to distinguish the instrument from the English horn. This is a brass instrument played by way of valves, that sounds a perfect fifth below the written note. See also *brass family; horn; transposing instrument.*

French horn

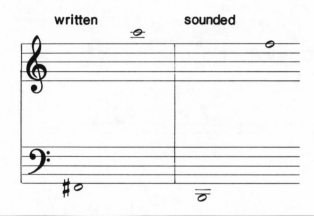

---

frentico   (It.) frenzied.

fret   strips of wood or metal that divide sections of certain stringed instruments into half-tone intervals. By depressing the strings between the frets, tones are altered, as the length of the vibrating string is shortened. See also *guitar; string family.*

freudig   (G.) joyfully.

frog   the section of a bow held in the performer's hand. See also *bow; string family.*

frottola   (It.) unaccompanied choral form. See also *choral; opera; vocal music.*

fugue

frusta (It.) see *whip.*

fugato (It.) an operatic passage or symphonic section performed in the style of a fugue. See also *opera; symphony; vocal music.*

fugue from the Latin *fuga,* or flight, a contrapuntal musical form in which a subject is introduced first in one voice or instrument, and then repeated in another. The introduction of this theme is called the exposition section. As themes are introduced in other voices, they appear in the dominant, or in the tonic in a different octave. The subject, or antecedent, is followed in this manner by the answer, or consequent. When the answer is identical to the subject, it is referred to as a real answer. Otherwise, it is a tonal answer. The development section follows the exposition, and then the resolution. See also *answer; antecedent; consequent; contrapuntal; countersubject; development; episode; exposition; imitation; real answer; resolution; round; subject; tonal answer.* See illustration, page 84.

full orchestra an orchestra at full force, with all four major sections: winds, brass, percussion and strings. In addition, the wind, brass and violin sections are usually divided into two separate parts. See also *orchestra.*

full organ instruction to play at full strength, but not necessarily using all stops. See also *organ; stop; volume.*

functional harmony forms of harmony that progress logically toward resolution. This logic is dictated by the combination of melody and bass line movement, and by natural sequencing of chords and harmony. See also *chord; harmony; non-functional harmony.*

---

functional harmony

fundamental **(1)** the root of a chord. **(2)** the note on which a harmonic series is founded. See also *chord; harmonic series; root.*

fundamental bass a series of roots in chords, whether actually sounded or not. When not sounded, the root is implied by the continuation of sound. If the bass consists entirely of fundamental tones, each bass note is also the root note, or tonic of the chord. See also *bass; chord; root; tonic.*

fundamental bass

furiex (Fr.) furiously.

furioso (It.) furiously.

G

gaiment (Fr.) gaily.

gaita (Sp.) see *bagpipe.*

galop a dance popular during the 19th century, played in duple time. See also *dance.*

gamelan an Asian orchestral ensemble of percussion instruments, often with the addition of strings and winds. See also *ensemble; orchestra; percussion family.*

gamut in its original use in Medieval times, the note G (*gamma ut*), the term later came to mean the entire range of the scale. See also *hexachord; range; scale.*

gapped scale   a scale containing intervals of more than whole tones, such as the pentatonic scale. See also *interval; pentatonic scale; scale.*

---

gapped scale

---

gavotte   a dance popular in 17th century France, often included as a movement in the Baroque suite. See also *Baroque; dance; suite.*

gebrauchsmusik   (G.) serious music easily played, due to its simple melody, harmonies, and rhythm. See also *character piece; exercise; salon music.*

gebunden   (G.) smoothly.

gehalten   (G.) sustained.

gehend   (G.) moderately.

geige   (G.) see *violin.*

general bass   a shorthand method of indicating the bass part of music, a system used during the Baroque period. See also *bass; figured bass; thorough bass.*

general pause   total silence, a rest of one or more full measures. Alt.—grand pause. See also *grand pause; notation; pause.*

gestopft   (G.) stopped (brass notation).

gigue   (Fr.) a fast dance in triple time that often opened with a fugue section, followed by an inversion of the same theme. The gigue often was used as the last movement in the Baroque suite. See also *Baroque; dance; jig; suite.*

giocoso   (It.) playfully.

gitarre   (G.) see *guitar.*

giusto   (It.) strictly to tempo.

glee   a short vocal composition for unaccompanied male voices, an outgrowth of the madrigal that was popular in England during the 17th and 18th centuries. See also *a cappella; madrigal; vocal music.*

glissando from the French word glisser, literally "to slide." However, the true glissando is not a slide, but a rapid depression of each note's value. Each whole or half tone is actually sounded in quick progression, within the defined range of the starting and ending notes. This is achievable on stringed and keyboard instruments. The glissando is often confused with the portamento, a rapidly executed gradual change in pitch, or a true slide on a stringed instrument. See also *portamento*.

glissando

glocken (G.) see *bells*.

glockenspiel a definite pitch percussion instrument consisting of a series of metal bars attached to a frame, in the same approximate order as a piano's keyboard. It is played with two small hand-held hammers. During the 18th century, the glockenspiel was played via a keyboard. See also *bells; keyboard instrument*.

glockenspiel

gong a definite pitch percussion instrument, made of a large bronze disk with slightly turned edge. It is suspended and struck with a hammer. The tone is deep and reverberating. The gong is often interchangably referred to as a tam-tam, with the usual distinction that the tam-tam is of indefinite pitch. See also *percussion family; tam-tam*.

Gothic period name assigned to music written from the mid-12th century through the mid-15th century, immediately preceding the Renaissance period. See also *Renaissance music*.

grace note   an ornamental note without time value, indicated by a small note with a diagonal line through its stem. The grace note appears immediately before the subject note, and is connected with a short tie. See also *ornament.*

---

grace note

---

gracieux   (Fr.) gracefully.

grand opera   **(1)** a serious or full-length opera, as oppossed to an operetta. **(2)** a musical production that is entirely sung, containing no spoken parts. **(3)** a large, spectacular production with elaborate sets, a chorus, and an historically significant plot. See also *opera; vocal music.*

grand pause   complete silence for one full measure or more, for all instruments in the orchestra. Alt.—general pause. See also *general pause; notation; pause.*

grand piano   a large piano with the soundboard placed horizontally. See also *piano; upright piano.*

grandioso   (It.) grandly.

grave   (It.) slowly and solemnly.

graziolo   (It.) gracefully.

great staff   the combined treble and bass clefs in a single set. See also *bass clef; treble clef.*

---

great staff

Greek modes ancient musical modes in use from approximately the 7th century B.C. through the second or third century A.D. These scales were thought of as declining, whereas the diatonic and Church modes are usually expressed in ascending order. Certain Church mode names were assigned to the Greek modes, although the Greek modes are not comparable to Church modes with the same names. See also *Church modes; mode; scale.*

Greek modes

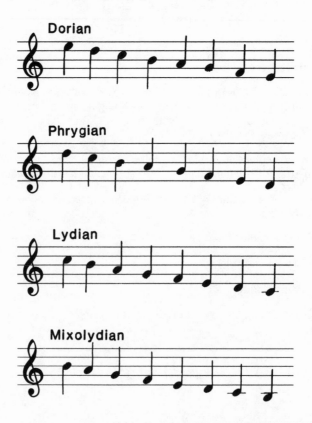

Gregorian chant a plainsong form of liturgical music, named for Pope Gergory I (c. 540–604). It is sung by a choir or comprised of a choir and soloists, completely in monophonic form and without consistent meter. The chants were written in what are now called Church modes, and approximately 3,000 are known to have been composed. None of the known chants are identified by composer, and were probably written by priests and monks. See also *chant; Church modes; monophonic sound; plainsong; vocal music.* See illustration, page 91.

Gregorian chant

ky - ri - e   e - le - i   -   son

Gregorian modes a distinction made by some music theorists, between authentic (Ambrosian) and Plagal (Gregorian) modes. This extended classification of Church modes recognizes that each authentic mode (with ranges beginning and ending on the tonic) has a related Plagal mode (with ranges beginning on the fourth degree below the tonic and ending on the fifth degree above):

authentic	*Plagal*
Dorian	Hypodorian
Phrygian	Hypophrygian
Lydian	Hypolydian
Mixolydian	Hypomixolydian

The authentic and Plagal modes are made by distinctions of range and ending note within a chant. These modes are not related in any sense to authentic or Plagal cadences. See also *Ambrosian chant; authentic mode; Church modes; mode; Plagal mode.* See illustration, page 92.

grelots (Fr.) see *sleigh bells.*

ground bass a four- to eight-measure bass line that is repeated continuously while the treble part plays variations on a theme. The form was popular in many Baroque compositions. See also *Baroque; bass; harmony.*

group any combination of performers, or the singers or instrumentalists required to perform a composition. See also *arrangement; ensemble; orchestration.*

guitar a stringed, fretted instrument used in pop and folk music. Several variations of the instrument exist, including bass and tenor versions. The most widely known and used is the six-string guitar, whose strings are tuned to E, A, D, G, B and E, and called the Spanish, or classical guitar. In pop music applications, the guitar often is electronic. Written music for guitar sounds one octave above the written note. However, in pop and folk music, it is common practice to substitute chord symbols for actual notes or harmonies, and leave it to performers to develop their own arrangements. See also *chord symbol; electronic instrument; finger board; folk music; fret; pop.* See illustration, page 92.

guitar chords symbols placed in a grid above the treble line, to assist guitar players, not only in which chord to play, but also in how to form the chord. The

Gregorian modes

Hypodorian (tonic D)

Hypophrygian (tonic E)

Hypolydian (tonic F)

Hypomixolydian (tonic G)

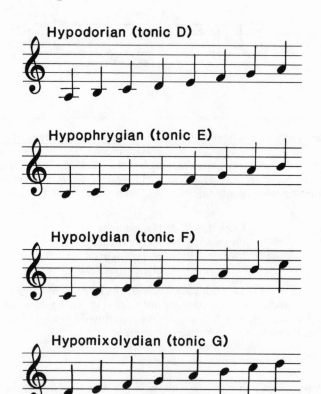

guitar

open strings:

name of the chord is also abbreviated above the chord symbol. The grid represents frets of the guitar (spaces between horizontal lines), and each of the strings (from the low E on the left to the high E on the right). Encoding includes:

depress—indicated by a black dot in the proper fret space and on the proper string's line.

leave open—indicated by a small, hollow circle placed above the appropriate string's line.

do not play—indicated by the absense of any symbols.

See also *chord symbol*.

guitar chords

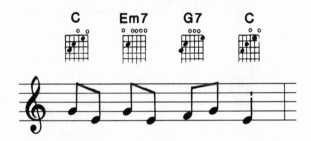

guitare   (Fr.) see *guitar*.

guitarra   (Sp.) see *guitar*.

gusto   (It.) with zest.

Gypsy scale   a scale employed to create the sound of Eastern European music, derived from music of the Gypsy culture. The second and sixth degrees are diminished. See also *scale*.

Gypsy scale

H

half cadence   a progression of chords with resolution to the dominant (fifth) tone or the subdominant (fourth) tone, but lacking the tonic chord. For example, in the key of C, a progression of a D chord, followed by a G chord, is a half cadence. See also *cadence; chord; dominant; imperfect cadence; subdominant; tonic.*

---

half cadence

---

half close   an imperfect cadence, or any progression of chords ending on a chord other than the tonic. See also *cadence; imperfect cadence.*

half note   a value represented by a written note symbol having half the value of a whole note. In 4/4 time, two half notes constitute a full measure, each having two beats. In 3/4 time, a whole note is worth two of the three beats in the measure, and a dotted half note is worth one full measure of three beats. See also **Illustrated Notation Guide.**

---

half note

half rest   a rest worth two beats. In 4/4 time, a half rest is worth two of the four beats in a measure. In 3/4 time, a half rest is equal to two of the three beats in a measure. See also **Illustrated Notation Guide.**

---

half rest

---

half step   the smallest interval in the chromatic scale, which consists of 12 equally measured half steps. In the diatonic major scale, notes are separated by whole steps, except between the 3rd and 4th degrees, and between the 7th and 8th degrees. These intervals are half steps. See also *chromatic scale; interval; whole tone.*

harfe   (G.) see *harp.*

harmonic analysis   the study of chords and harmony in composition, including the labeling of chords by degree (tonic, dominant, subdominant, etc.) and by inversion. See also *chord; interval; inversion.*

harmonic inversion   **(1)** the movement of note positions within a chord, without substituting any note values, so that the same chord is sounded, but in different sequence. **(2)** the substitution of parts in one voice for another. For example, a bass part is introduced and, in the development, is repeated in the top voice. See also *chord; inversion; invertible counterpoint.* See illustration, page 96.

harmonic minor scale   a variation of the minor scale, in which the third and sixth degrees are diminished. See also *diatonic; melodic minor scale; minor scale; natural minor scale;* and **Scales, Keys and Chords.** See illustration, page 96.

harmonic rhythm   a measurement of the degree and frequency of change in a composition's harmony. The speed of performance and number of chords do not affect the harmonic rhythm. A "slow" rhythm is one in which a repetitive bass or repeated and inverted single chords last for several measures. A "fast"

harmonic inversion

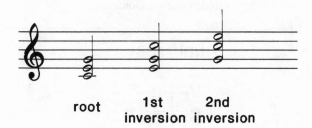

root   **1st**   **2nd**
inversion inversion

---

harmonic minor scale

---

harmonic rhythm is one in which the harmony is altered frequently. See also *chord; fundamental; interval; rhythm.*

harmonic scale   see *harmonic minor scale.*

harmonic series   the related sounds that result when any single note is sounded, also called partials. The series accounts for the individual characteristics and tone color associated with the voice or any particular instrument. Every instrument produces sounds that are distinguishable from other types of instruments, and has its own harmonic strengths or weaknesses. If the harmonic series could be filtered out, a single tone would have a flat quality, and every instrument would sound identical.

The harmonic series can be either reduced or enhanced in electronic sound reproduction, through tone control filtering. However, a pure elimination of the harmonics would not be desirable. Although the human ear is not aware of the secondary sounds, it is the combination of the note and the harmonic series that is identified as a particular note, performed by a particular instrument.

Calculated from any sounded note, called the fundamental, the notes in the harmonic series have a precise mathematical relationship in sounds higher than the sounded note. It must be remembered, however, that the notes played in the diatonic scale are estimated interval values between perfect intervals, and are not completely accurate. Thus, the higher the harmonic series progresses, the farther the pure mathematical relationship varies from notes that can be played on a diatonically tuned instrument.

The harmonic relationships, assigned by numbers beginning with 1 (for the fundamental) are:

Position	Interval
1 to 2	octave
2 to 3	perfect fifth
3 to 4	perfect fourth
4 to 5	major third
5 to 6	minor third

As the series progresses, relationships of the harmonic series take on fractionally smaller intervals. The 16th position is four octaves above the fundamental. See also *fundamental; interval; overtone; partial; sympathetic vibration; tone color.*

---

harmonic series

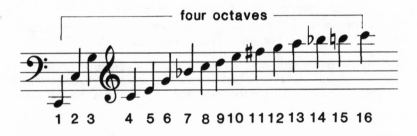

harmonica   a small, hand-held wind instrument of rectangular shape. A series of air holes are connected to reeds in the center of the instrument, which vibrate when air is exhaled or inhaled by the player. The tonal quality can be muted by cupping the escape of air with the hand. Single notes can be sounded, although the harmonica is more often used to produce chords. This is not considered an orchestral instrument, but has been used widely in both jazz and popular music. It is an inflexible instrument, tuned in a single key. Some harmonicas are equipped with a button that can be used to play accidentals. However, a complete modulation to a secondary key would be difficult, impossible if the performer desired to play chords. See also *jazz; pop; wind family.*

harmonics   (1) the tone produced as part of a harmonic series. (2) In more common application, the tones produced on a stringed instrument by lightly touching a vibrating open string, rather than fully depressing it (a natural harmonic) or touching a stopped string (an artificial harmonic). Notation to perform a harmonic is indicated with a small, hollow circle above the note to be sounded.

Harmonics can also be produced on the flute by overblowing, or on brass instruments for those notes sounded without the use of valves. The note value of the harmonic will vary depending on the position at which the string is touched. See also *overtone; string family.* See illustration, page 98.

harmonics

notation

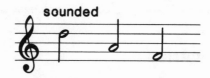

sounded

---

harmonium   an organ-like instrument on which vibrations are produced by operation of a bellows. See also *keyboard instrument; reed.*

harmony   a combination of tones within chords, to produce mood through tonal relationships, consonance or dissonance. Harmony is the vertical relationship in music, while melody is the horizontal. See also *chord; interval; texture.*

---

harp

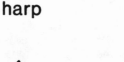

octave
higher

---

harp   a large stringed orchestral instrument. Most models contain 45 strings in a triangular wooden frame. The harp is tuned in C flat. Foot pedals enable the performer to either sharpen or flatten notes. When the pedal is depressed, the change occurs for all strings of that note value. The harp has poor volume but a clear and rich tone color, especially in its middle range. It is well suited for the playing of chords, either singularly or in a roll; single notes; arpeggios; diatonic scales; and the glissando. However, complex and fast chromatic variations are not possible on the harp, due to the need to operate the foot pedals for each change. See also *string family*. See illustration, page 98.

harpe (Fr.) see *harp.*

harpsichord a keyboard instrument popular from the 16th to the 18th centuries. It is distinguished from the piano and clavichord in the method of producing sounds. The harpsichord's strings are plucked by quill or leather tongues, operated mechancially from the keyboard. Sound cannot be varied by touch, as it can on the piano, but can be controlled to a degree by operation of foot pedals and manuals. See also *clavichord; piano; spinet; string family; virginal.*

---

harpsichord

---

hautbois (Fr.) see *oboe.*

head voice the registration in vocal music in the upper ranges, where vibration occurs in the singer's head rather than in the chest. See also *register; vocal music.*

hemidemisemiquaver the British name for the 64th note, which is indicated by a four-flagged stem, or by four bars. See also *sixty-fourth note;* and **Illustrated Notation Guide.** See illustration, page 100.

hemiola (alt. hemiolia, hemiole) "one and one half," a term used in the 16th century to denote a change in note value, usually going from three to two. For example, 6/4 time reverts to 3/2. See also *notation; rhythm.*

hemidemisemiquaver

flag　　　　bar

---

heterophony　a primitive polyphonic form of music in which two or more performers played the same melody, but with subtle changes and variations. Notes were added, excluded, or substituted, or short improvised passages were added to the music as written. See also *improvisation; polyphony.*

hexachord　any grouping of six tones, each separated by a whole tone between the first three and the second three degrees; and by a half tone between the 3rd and 4th degrees. The hexachord formed the basis for the original fasola system. In the key of C, two hexachords exist:

　　C-D-E-F-G-A
　　G-A-B-C-D-E

By adding B flat, a third hexachord is created:

　　F-G-A-Bb-C-D

See also *chord; degree; fasola; scale; solmization; tetrachord.*

---

hexachord

half
tone

---

hexatonic scale　a scale with six distinct notes in the span of one octave, rather than the eight found in the modern diatonic scale. The development of the hexatonic scale followed the five-tone (pentatonic) scale, and preceded the diatonic. Either the fourth or the seventh degree is excluded. See also *diatonic; pentatonic scale.* See illustration, page 101.

hidden fifth　an interval relationship consisting of two consecutive perfect fifth

hexatonic scale

without the 4th

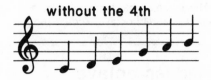

without the 7th

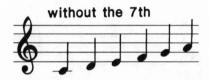

intervals, resulting from the similar motion in the various voices or parts of a composition. The parallel, or consecutive fifth is considered a flaw in traditional theory and for composition prior to the 20th century. Parallel motion creating the "hidden" fifth is the result of motion in dissimilar voices. For example, in the first chord, the top note is G and the bottom note is C. This relationship is a perfect fifth. In the second chord, the second voice ascends to note A and the bottom voice ascends to D. This creates a second perfect fifth interval. But because the result does not occur consecutively in the same parts, but rather is the result of similar motion, the fifths are hidden. See also *consecutive interval; fifth; interval; parallel fifths; similar motion.*

hidden fifth

hidden octave   a parallel octave created by similar motion in different parts. Voices move from one chord to another, with the flawed parallel octave resulting. All consecutive perfect intervals are considered as flaws in pre–20th century music. Example: In the first chord, the second voice and the fourth voice both sound the note C. In the second chord, the top voice and the bottom voice both descend to G. This creates a hidden parallel octave. See also *consecutive interval; interval; octave; parallel octave; similar motion.*

hidden octave

homophonic sound   a simple voice or melody line, supported only by chords. See also *monophonic sound; polyphony.*

homophonic sound

horn   **(1)** the abbreviated name of the horn in F, a transposing brass instrument also called the French horn, to distinguish it from the English horn. **(2)** in jazz ensembles, any brass instrument, including the trumpet, trombone and sax-ophone. See also *brass family; French horn.*

horn fifth   parallel chords or voices purposely written for multiple brass parts in orchestration. The term is not restricted to perfect fifth intervals, but applies to any consecutive interval played on a natural horn. See also *parallel fifths; trumpet.*

horn fifth

hurdy-gurdy **(1)** an obsolete mechanical viol, the strings of which were vibrated by a hand-operated wheel, rather than with a bow. Notes were sounded by the other hand, by means of a small keyboard instead of directly depressing strings. **(2)** a term used to inaccurately describe any instrument on which sound is produced by the operation of a handle or turning wheel. See also *string family.*

hurtig   (G.) quickly.

hymn   a song praising a deity, or of a patriotic nature. See also *anthem; song; vocal music.*

Hypodorian mode   a Plagal variation of the Dorian mode, with a range from the fourth degree below to the fifth degree above the tonic note D. See also *Church modes; Dorian mode; Plagal mode.*

Hypodorian mode

Hypolydian mode   a Plagal variation of the Lydian mode, with a range from the fourth degree below to the fifth degree above the tonic note F. See also *Church modes; Lydian mode; Plagal mode.* See illustration, page 104.

Hypolydian mode

Hypomixolydian mode a Plagal variation of the Mixolydian mode, with a range from the fourth degree below to the fifth degree above the tonic note G. See also *Church modes; Mixolydian mode; Plagal mode.*

Hypomixolydian mode

Hypophrygian mode a Plagal variation of the Phrygian mode, with a range from the fourth degree below to the fifth degree above the tonic note E. See also *Church modes; Phrygian mode; Plagal mode.*

Hypophrygian mode

I

idiom a style, format or method of playing that is especially well suited to a particular instrument. For example, the glissando is idiomatic for the violin, but not for the oboe. See also *instrumentation; style.*

idiophone any instrument that can be sounded by moving or striking, generally applied to percussion instruments. See also *membranophone.*

imitation   the exact, approximate or derived repeating of a theme, either in the same key or in a related key. The fugue and canon make use of imitation, and development sections of compositions use imitation in many forms. See also *answer; canon; counterpoint; development; motive (motif); subject; theme; variation.*

imperfect cadence   a cadence consisting of a dominant chord followed by the tonic, as in a perfect cadence. However, in an imperfect cadence, the tonic note does not appear in the top voice. See also *cadence; perfect cadence; root; tonic.*

imperfect cadence

impressionism   a term originally applied to art and literature, describing a movement toward subtle, soft message and tone, color, and understatement of emotions. In music, the term describes works in the style of Debussy. Impressionistic music was popular from approximately 1890 until 1915. It is considered by some as a transition from the Romantic period to the Modern. By others, it is thought to be a brief period of its own. See also *expressionism; Modern period; Romantic music.*

impromptu   (Fr.) a short composition, usually for piano, that suggests a free, even improvised style. See also *character piece.*

improvisation   the creation of music or harmony spontaneously and not in accordance with a written score. Improvisation includes the free thorough bass and use of ornamentation. In Modern music, improvisation is associated with jazz. See also *extemporization; jazz; thorough bass.*

incidental music   music written as a bridge between acts in a play, or as background to dialogue or unspoken segments in a production. See also *interlude; orchestration.*

indefinite pitch clef   the clef used for percussion instruments, that provide rhythmic additions to music. It consists of two vertical bars in place of a clef sign. See also *clef; percussion family;* and **Illustrated Notation Guide.**

---

indefinite pitch clef

---

inner voices   in vocal music, the alto and tenor parts. When arranged from top to bottom, four-part vocal scores appear in the order of soprano, alto, tenor and bass. Thus, inner voices are on the second and third lines. See also *outer voices, vocal music.*

innig   (G.) fervently.

instrumentation   the selection and combination of instruments in a composition's score. See also *arrangement; orchestration; score.*

interlude   music that acts as bridge between movements, or in a play, between acts. See also *incidental music.*

intermezzo   (It.) **(1)** see *interlude.* **(2)** a short comic opera of the 18th century, with a limited number of scenes and characters. **(3)** a short composition for piano. **(4)** a strictly instrumental section in an opera that connects two acts or scenes. See also *character piece; comic opera; opera.*

interpretation   **(1)** one performer's version of a composition, based on either a belief about the composer's true intentions, or a variation based on the performer's individual expression. **(2)** a rearrangement, reorchestration, transcription or other change to an existing composition, which alters the original composer's intent. See also *transcription; variation.*

interval   the pitch difference between two degrees of the scale. The modern diatonic scale consists of 12 half tones per octave, and whole tones (equal to two half tones).
   An interval is measured from the lower of any two pitches, a note called the prime. The number of degrees separating the two determines the interval and its name. When two notes are identical, there is no true interval. However, this relationship is referred to as a "perfect prime" interval.
   Major, minor and perfect intervals may be simple or compound. A simple interval is one with a degree difference of one octave or less. These include:

name	sounded notes	number of half tones
minor second	C−D♭	1
major second	C−D	2

interval

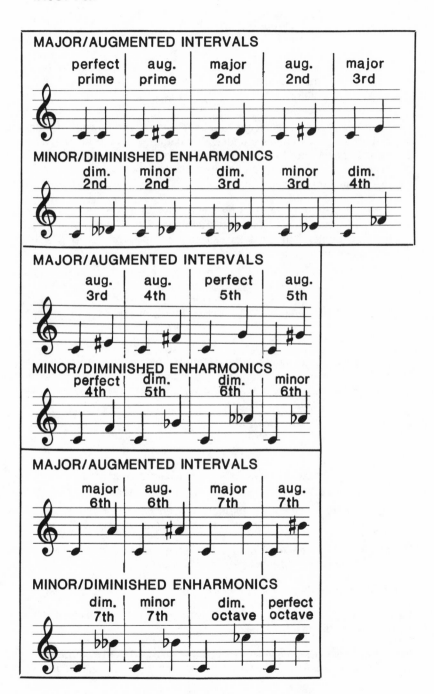

minor third	C−E♭	3
major third	C−E	4
perfect fourth	C−F	5
perfect fifth	C−G	7
minor sixth	C−A♭	8
major sixth	C−A	9
minor seventh	C−B♭	10
major seventh	C−B	11
octave	C−C	12

Any interval can be augmented (raised) or diminished (lowered) by altering one or both of the two notes sounded. The names of such octaves depend on the value of the prime. Every interval has an enharmonic equivalent.

Example: A major third can be augmented so that notes C and E# (F) are sounded. While this interval is identical to a perfect fourth, it is also the enharmonic augmented third.

Example: A perfect fifth can be augmented so that notes C and G# are sounded. This interval is identical to the minor sixth (C and Ab).

Intervals greater than one octave are called compound intervals. Each consists of two or more simple intervals:

compound interval	combination
ninth	octave plus a second
tenth	octave plus a third
eleventh	octave plus a fourth
twelfth	octave plus a fifth

Each upward interval has a downward complement, or inversion, created by moving the lower tone up one octave; or by moving the higher tone down one octave. The difference in value of inverted intervals is always one octave:

notes	interval	notes	interval
C−D	second	D−C	seventh
C−E	third	E−C	sixth
C−F	fourth	F−C	fifth
C−G	fifth	G−C	fourth
C−A	sixth	A−C	third
C−B	seventh	B−C	second

See also *compound interval; enharmonic; inversion; major interval; minor interval; perfect interval; simple interval.* See illustration, page 107.

intonation   the quality of pitch, a judgment about how close a tone is to the exact pitch. See also *just intonation; pitch.*

intrepido   (It.) boldly.

introduction   the beginning section of a composition, in which the main theme is sounded for the first time. See also *theme.*

invention   a two- or three-voice composition for a keyboard instrument, similar to the fugue but less strictly formed. See also *counterpoint; fugue; round; voice.*

inversion   (1) the alteration of a chord from one position to another. Example: In the root position, the tonic is in the base. In the first inversion, the third is in the bass. (2) the interval that is related to another interval when the higher note is moved down one octave, or when the lower note is moved up one octave. Example: In the key of C, a perfect fifth consists of notes C and G. The inversion of this chord is a perfect fourth, consisting of notes G and C. (3) see *invertible counterpoint*. (4) the modification of a theme in which all ascending notes become descending, and all descending notes become ascending. See also *chord; counterpoint; fugue; interval; position*. See illustration, page 110.

inversion (chord)

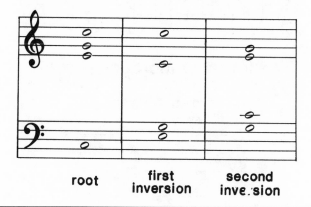

root   **first** **second**
              inversion **inve:sion**

inversion (interval)

perfect **perfect**
fifth **fourth**

inverted mordent   notation to play two or more ornaments, or a short trill. The exact number of notes played is dependent upon the tempo at the time the mordent appears. Although the exact meaning of a mordent depends on the musical period, prevailing practice, and country, it is generally considered to begin and end on the higher of two notes. The inverted mordent begins and ends on the lower note. It is usually written out rather than indicated by notation. See also *mordent; notation; trill; turn*. See illustration, page 110.

inversion (theme)

original

inverted

inverted mordent

mordent   **inverted**

invertible counterpoint the transposition of contrapuntal parts, so that lower and upper voices are reversed. See also *counterpoint; double counterpoint.*

invertible counterpoint

theme

inverted

Ionian mode   a mode added to the original Church modes of Dorian, Phrygian, Lydian and Mixolydian. The Ionian, devised in the 16th century, begins and ends on the tonic C and is identical to the modern diatonic scale. See also *Church modes; mode.*

Ionian mode

irregular grouping   any combination of notes not consistent with the meter in effect. Most common of these is the triplet (performance of three equally timed notes in the meter space of either two or four beats). See also *duplet; quadruplet; quintuplet; septuplet; sextuplet; triplet.*

irregular grouping

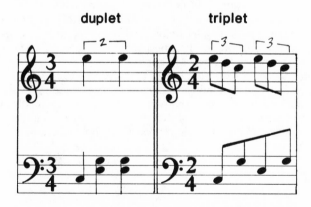

isorhythm   a system of composition used in the 14th and 15th centuries. A fixed rhythmic pattern remained throughout several sections of the same work. See also *cantus firmus; motet.*

istesso tempo   (It.) the same tempo.

J

jam the improvisation of melody and harmony, involving both soloists and an ensemble, in jazz music. See also *improvisation.*

jazz music derived from ragtime, popularized in the United States during the 20th century. Improvisation is an essential characteristic of jazz, which is usually written in duple meter and employs complex rhythm and syncopation. Jazz ensembles include brass and rhythm instruments. See also *bebop; blues; jive; ragtime; swing.*

jeu de timbres (Fr.) see *glockenspiel.*

jig (1) alternate spelling of gigue. (2) a dance popular in 16th century England, of a fast and often light nature. See also *dance; gigue.*

jive a fast-tempo improvisation in jazz music. See also *improvisation; jazz.*

just intonation (1) natural temperament, which can be performed on stringed instruments and by voice, but not by any instrument confined to the equally distributed pitch values of the diatonic scale.

The theory of just intonation is based on the premise that the third and fifth degrees of the scale are pure, and all other tones are derivitives of those degrees. The equal temperament system in use today has a division of 12 equal parts per octave. This facilitates consistent tuning and harmonic relationships in many keys. With just intonation, keys farthest removed from the justly tuned key would be progressively less exact in pitch.

(2) a theory promoted by some string players and vocalists that enharmonic tones can be distinguished, and that performance of those tones should have different values. Example: An F sharp is approximately one-tenth of a whole tone higher in value than the G flat. A minor distinction such as this cannot be heard by most human ears. See also *enharmonic; equal temperament; intonation; temperament.*

K

kettledrum see *tympani.*

key (1) in tonal music, the center or primary note that identifies the tonic. Thus, in the key of C, the note C is the tonic, whether that key is major or minor. (2) part of the action of the piano and other keyboard instruments. When the key is struck, it activates a hammer, which in turn strikes the string to produce a vibration. (3) metal levers on wind instruments that open or close air holes and vary the pitch. See also *accidental; action; piano; tonality; wind family.*

key color   the belief of some musicians that each key has its own, individual character or mood. Many composers have favored certain keys. However, it is more likely that the choice was made in consideration of performance quality in upper and lower voice or instrument ranges, and the sound quality of the chord range. See also *range*.

key relationship   the progressive tonal changes from one key to another, which is best observed in a comparison of key signatures. By adding or subtracting sharps and flats from any key signature, the related keys are identified:

relationship	*key signature changes*
key of the dominant	add one sharp or subtract one flat
key of the subdominant	subtract one sharp or add one flat.

In addition to interval and key signature relationship, keys are further related by major and minor modes. The related minor keys have the same key signatures as the major key one and one-half steps above. Example: the key of A minor has the same key signature as that of C major. See also *circle of fifths; common chord; relative key.*

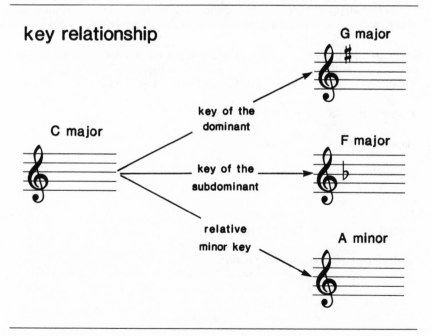

key relationship

key signature   the symbol made up of sharps or flats at the left side of each line of music, showing the key in which the music is to be played or sung. See also **Scales, Keys and Chords.**

keyboard **(1)** any instrument that is played by striking or depressing keys. **(2)** on a keyboard instrument, the row of white and black keys. See also *organ; piano.*

---

keyboard

---

keyboard harmony the addition of figured bass, progressions of chords, harmonization of melodies, modulation, and improvisation, as practiced on the piano, organ and other keyboard instruments. As opposed to a composition skill, keyboard harmony is an ability developed through practice, and is used to teach students to improve their familiarity with the theory of harmony. See also *chord; figured bass; harmony; improvisation; modulation.*

keyboard instrument any instrument that is played via keys, operated by hand alone (such as the piano) or by both hands and feet (the organ, for example). See also *clavichord; harmonium; harpsichord; organ; piano.*

klapper (G.) see *rattle.*

klapphörnchen (G.) see *cornet.*

klarinette (G.) see *clarinet.*

klavier (G.) see *piano.*

kontrabass (G.) see *double bass.*

kontrafagott (G.) see *contrabassoon.*

L

lah the sixth degree of the scale, in the solmization system. See also *degree; solmization; submediant.*

lament   a composition intended to convey sorrow, written to be performed at a funeral. See also *dirge; requiem.*

langsam   (G.) slowly.

larghetto   (It.) very broadly.

larghissimo   (It.) extremely broadly.

largo   (It.) broadly.

látigo   (Sp.) see *whip.*

laúd   (Sp.) see *lute.*

laute   (G.) see *lute.*

leading motif   a theme that represents a character, mood, or emotion, from the German word leitmotif. The term was first used in descriptions of themes written in operas by Wagner. See also *leitmotif; motive (motif); opera; theme.*

leading seventh   the minor seventh chord, which often precedes (thus, leads into) the tonic resolution. The minor seventh degree of the dominant chord is the leading seventh. An essential part of the chord is the leading tone, that note a half step lower than the tonic (the third degree in the dominant chord). This resolves to the tonic directly under accepted rules of harmony. Example: In the key of C, the leading seventh is the G minor seventh chord, and the note B resolves to the tonic C. See also *dominant; seventh; tonic.*

leading seventh

leading tone   the seventh degree of the diatonic scale, also called the subtonic. In the major mode, the leading tone is the note a half step lower than the tonic. See also *degree; diatonic; semitone; subtonic.*

leap   a change in notes of more than a whole step. When notes change in progression from one diatonic step to another, the result is conjunct motion. Any departure from this is a leap. See also *conjunct; diatonic.*

leap

lebhaft   (G.) lively.

ledger lines   (alt. leger lines) lines written outside of the five staff lines, to record notes above or below the staff range. See also *range; staff;* and **Illustrated Notation Guide.**

ledger lines

legatissimo   (It.) very smoothly.

legato   (It.) smoothly.

leggiero   (It.) lightly.

leier   (G.) see *lyre.*

leitmotif   (G.) see *leading motif.*

lentissimo   (It.) extremely slowly.

lento (It.) slowly.

letter notation alphabetical names assigned to the various pitches, A through G. These are written out to indicate chords, with letter notation written above the melody line; or, in music for beginners, as an aid in learning to read music. See also *pitch names*.

---

letter notation

G   D C   B   D

---

libretto (It.) "booklet," the words and script of an opera, musical comedy, or other musical work. See also *lyric; musical comedy; opera*.

licenza (It.) at liberty.

lieblich (G.) sweetly.

lied (G.) song.

ligature **(1)** a band used to stabilize a reed onto the mouthpiece of wind and brass instruments. **(2)** a form of notation first used in 12th century plainsong composition, to specify notes and rhythmic mode. As in mensural notation, the lack of measure bars required an elaborate code for proper rhythm. Ligature was the forerunner of the notation system in use today. See also *mensural music; neumes; plainsong; rhythmic mode; slur*. See illustration, page 118.

light music any form of music for a limited ensemble, or intended to be performed on a small scale. Many operettas belong in this classification. See also *operetta*.

light opera see *operetta*.

line **(1)** a part or voice in music, when compared to other lines to be sounded at the same time. **(2)** see *ledger lines*. **(3)** the quality of continuity in music. Example: a "long" line indicates smoothness and a seemingly effortless harmony and combination of sound. **(4)** the general direction or pattern of a melody or part. At a particular point in a composition, a part may rise (an ascending line) or fall (a descending line). See also *harmony; melody; part; voice*.

ligature

---

linear counterpoint   a form of counterpoint in which each part maintains its own individuality, even while part of the harmonic whole. This term is applied both to the compositions of Bach, and to modern composition trends. See also *counterpoint; harmony.*

lira   (It.) (Sp.) see *lyre.*

liturgical music   any form of music originally composed to be performed as part of a worship service, or intended to convey religious expression. Western music has been influenced greatly by liturgical music of the Christian church. See also *Ambrosian chant; Anglican chant; Church modes; Gregorian chant.*

liuto   (It.) see *lute.*

loco   (It.) return to octave as written.

Locrian mode   a theortical Church mode consisting of the natural tones beginning and ending on the note B. It is not a practical mode because it lacks a perfect fifth degree. See also *Church modes; mode.* See illustration, page 119.

Locrian mode

---

log drum   a cylindrical, wooden drum sealed at both ends, with gaps or slits along its sides. The log drum is a definite pitch instrument. See also *drum; percussion family.*

lourd   (Fr.) heavily.

lullaby   a song intended to soothe, to be played softly. The term usually is applied to vocal music only, but also has been used for instrumental compositions. See also *song; vocal music.*

lunga pausa   (It.) long pause.

lustig   (G.) merrily.

lute   a stringed, fretted instrument with a pear-shaped body, popular in the 16th and 17th centuries, and again in the 20th century. The right hand plucks strings (or a plectrum can be used), while the left hand depresses strings in frets. Much of the lute music of the past was composed using the tablature notation system (which gave placement of the left hand's fingers on specific strings and frets, rather than direct notation or chords). Tuning of strings varies between versions of the instrument's size and by region. The most common open string tuning, from the lowest to the highest strings, is: G, C, F, A, D and G. See also *mandolin; plectrum; string family; tablature.*

---

lute

open strings

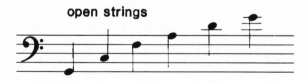

---

luth   (Fr.) see *lute.*

Lydian mode   a Church mode represented by the natural tones beginning and ending on the note F. See also *Church modes; mode.* See illustration, page 120.

Lydian mode

---

lyre (alt. lira) **(1)** a Greek stringed instrument whose body is made of turtle shell, with wooden arms each containing strings and connected by a crossbeam. **(2)** a percussion instrument similar to the glockenspiel, but in the shape of the stringed lyre. **(3)** a clip used to attach sheets of music to instruments, used in military and marching bands. See also *band; glockenspiel; percussion family; string family.*

lyric **(1)** the words of a song or the words that are accompanied by music in a stage performance. **(2)** a voice of intermediate quality and weight, usually applied to tenor and soprano only. **(3)** a lyric dance, or opera. **(4)** descriptive of music the composer considered as poetic, or based on a poem. See also *opera; song; vocal music.*

M

madrigal **(1)** Italian vocal music of the 14th through 16 centuries, written as duets or trios. The form included two (sometimes three) stanzas of identical music, followed by a final stanza (form AAB). **(2)** four-part vocal music in England during the 16th and 17th centuries, similar to the motet but of a secular nature. The madrigal usually was performed a cappella, while some were written with instrumental parts. **(3)** descriptive of certain songs in operettas, in which two or more performers imitate the madrigal style. See also *a cappella; counterpoint; motet; operetta; vocal music.*

maestoso (It.) majestic.

maggiore (It.) major (key).

majeur (Fr.) major (key).

major interval an interval of the 2nd, 3rd, 6th or 7th degrees. If reduced a half tone, the major interval becomes minor. If reduced two half tones, it becomes a diminished interval. And if raised a half tone, it becomes an augmented interval. A major chord is transferred into minor, diminished or augmented by changing one or more of its interval degrees. The 4th, 5th and 8th (octave) degrees are not major, but perfect intervals. In the key of C, the major intervals are:

Interval	Notes
Major 2nd	C–D
Major 3rd	C–E
Major 6th	C–A
Major 7th	C–B

See also *augmented chord; diminished chord; interval; minor interval; perfect interval.*

major interval

major scale the diatonic scale, consisting of whole tones between each degree, except for the 3rd to 4th and the 7th to 8th degrees, which are half tones. The relationship is identical in every key:

degree

Key	1	2	3	4	5	6	7	8
C	C	D	E	F	G	A	B	C
C♯	C♯	D♯	E♯	F♯	G♯	A♯	B♯	C♯
D	D	E	F♯	G	A	B	C♯	D
E♭	E♭	F	G	A♭	B♭	C	D	E
E	E	F♯	G♯	A	B	C♯	D♯	E
F	F	G	A	B♭	C	D	E	F
F♯	F♯	G♯	A♯	B	C♯	D♯	E♯	F
G	G	A	B	C	D	E	F♯	G
A♭	A♭	B♭	C	D♭	E♭	F	G	A♭
A	A	B	C♯	D	E	F♯	G♯	A
B♭	B♭	C	D	E♭	F	G	A	B♭
B	B	C♯	D♯	E	F♯	G♯	A♯	B

See also *diatonic; minor scale; scale; tetrachord.*

major scale

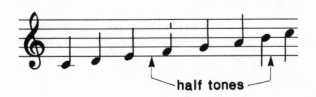

half tones

mallet   a rubber-headed tool used for playing certain keyboard percussion instruments. See also *glockenspiel; percussion family; vibraphone; xylophone.*

mandola   (G.) see *mandolin.*

mandolin   a stringed, fretted instrument developed from the lute. It is played with a plectrum, and has four sets of double strings. Tuning in the most widely used versions is in fifths, identical to the tuning of a violin's open strings. See also *lute; plectrum; string family.*

---

mandolin

open strings

---

mandolina   (Sp.) see *mandolin.*

mandoline   (Fr.) see *mandolin.*

mandolino   (It.) See also *mandolin.*

manual keyboard   a keyboard played with the hands, as compared to the pedal keyboard of the organ, which is played with the feet. See also *keyboard; organ; pedal; piano.*

manuscript   music written out by hand, or paper printed with staffs and key signatures. See also *orchestration; score.*

maraca   (Sp.) see *rattle.*

marcato   (It.) marked, to be played with emphasis. See also *accent; notation.*

march   music in 4/4 time, usually emphasizing the first beat, with recurring four-measure phrases. The march often is military in nature, and is played by marching bands, although march movements also are found in orchestral music. See also *band; orchestra.*

marimba   an instrument similar to the xylophone, but with a range expanded up to six octaves. It is played with muted, soft-headed sticks. See also *mute; percussion family; xylophone.*

marziale   (It.) in the style of a march.

masculine cadence   the name given to a cadence that ends on a strong beat. In comparison, a feminine cadence is one ending on a weak beat. See also *cadence; feminine cadence.*

---

masculine cadence

---

masculine theme   the stronger or more prominent of two themes in the sonata form. In comparison, a feminine theme is the secondary one, usually appearing in the middle of a movement. See also *feminine theme; sonata form; ternary form; theme.*

mass   the Roman Catholic worship service. The musical representation of the mass has two parts: the proper and the ordinary. Each contains distinct music and text:

proper	*ordinary*
introit	kyrie
gradual	gloria
alleluia	credo
offertory	santus
communion	agnus Dei

See also *liturgical music; organum; plainsong.*

mazurka   a Polish folk dance performed by four couples (sometimes eight). It is written in triple time, with emphasis on the second or third beat, and is characterized by dotted rhythms. See also *dance; folk music; triple time.*

mean tones   a toning system with unequal temperament, closer to values found in pure harmonics. The system was used in the 16th through 18th centuries, but was not practical for keys that were more than three sharps or flats removed from the centrally tuned key. See also *temperament; unequal temperament.*

measure a recognizable grouping of beats, set off by bar lines. Distinguishing measures make it possible to read music in a continuous line, track tempo and meter, and coordinate performance with other instrumentalists or singers. See also *bar line; meter; notation;* and **Illustrated Notation Guide.**

measure

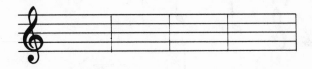

mechanical instrument any instrument that creates or reproduces music, without the need for a player. The carillon and player piano are examples. See also *carillon; piano.*

medesimo tempo (It.) in the same tempo.

mediant the third degree of the scale, located midway between the tonic and the dominant. See also *degree; interval; scale; tone.*

mediant

medium a specific instrument, ensemble, voice, or combination of performers. Compositions are written with the medium in mind. This determines the idiomatic and tonal limitations. See also *idiom; instrumentation; orchestration; part; voice.*

medley a loosely constructed series of songs or short instrumental pieces, often performed together as though a single composition. See also *composition; song.*

melodic minor scale a variation of the minor scale. In comparison to the major scale, melodic minor is constructed in the following way: The third degree is lowered one half step when ascending; when descending, the 6th and 7th degrees are also lowered. Example: In the key of C major, there are no sharps or flats. The ascending melodic minor scale is C, D, E♭, F, G, A, B, C. The descending version is C, B♭, A♭, G, F, E♭, D, C. When the melodic minor is expressed in terms of its key signature, the explanation is different. Example: the key signature for C minor has three flats, B, A and E. The ascending melodic minor involves raising the 6th and 7th degrees from values indicated by key signature. When descending, the 6th and 7th degrees are played as dictated by the key signature. See also *harmonic minor scale; minor scale; natural minor scale;* and **Scales, Keys and Chords.**

melodic minor scale

ascending

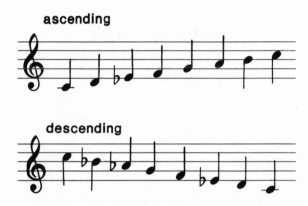

descending

melodrama   spoken passages in stage performances, accompanied by music. This is not the same as the non-musical dramatic form, melodrama, which is not a musical production. In the musical sense, melodrama is the spoken word with background music. In a musical comedy or operetta, musical sections contrast with spoken sections. See also *musical comedy; operetta.*

melody   the combination of tones that, when given rhythm, constitutes the vertical movement of music. The third element, that of harmony, is horizontal movement. When added together, the melody/rhythm and harmony constitute the complete texture of music. See also *harmony; movement; rhythm; texture.*

melody range   the range of pitches suitable for performance of the melody, generally thought to extend from the G below middle C to two octaves above middle C. See also *range.* See illustration, page 126.

membranophone   a classification of instruments sounded by striking a stretched skin, or membrane; drums. See also *drum; idiophone; percussion family.*

mensural music   a system of notation in use from the 13th through 17th centuries, that preceded modern notation. The system lacked measures, and

melody range

---

substituted long values to certain notes. See also *ligature; neumes; notation systems.*

---

mensural music

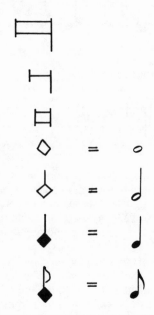

---

mesto   (It.) sadly.

meter   (alt. metre) the pulse, or beat of music. The term often is used inaccurately to describe rhythm, which is the timing and pattern of notes. Meter is indicated by the time signature, showing the number and type of note per measure. See also *beat; rhythm; time signature.*

meter notation   the time signature used in music, instructing the performer as to the correct meter. The upper number is the count of beats per measure, and the lower is the type of note. This is *not* a fraction, although one number appears above the other. Example: 3/4 meter is three-quarter notes per measure. And 3/8 meter specifies three eighth notes per measure. See also *key signature;* and **Illustrated Notation Guide.**

metronome   a device used to measure tempo, patented in 1814. It consists of a pendulum that swings back and forth, ticking on each beat. The speed is reduced by raising a weight on the pendulum, and increased by lowering the weight. The metronome is operated by winding, like a clock. Some battery-operated and electric models have also been manufactured. See also *meter; tempo.*

metronome mark   a note placed above the staff at the beginning of a composition, or at the point that the tempo changes. It shows the exact number of beats to be performed per minute. See also *beat; tempo.*

metronome mark

mezzo forte (mf)   (It.) moderately loud.

mezzo piano (mp)   (It.) moderately soft.

mezzo soprano   (It.) female voice approximately midway between the soprano and alto ranges. See also *alto; soprano; voice.*

mezzo soprano

mi   the third degree of the diatonic scale, in the solmization system. See also *degree; mediant; solmization.*

middle C   the C note approximately halfway on the piano keyboard, and written on the first ledger line below the treble clef, or on the first ledger line above the bass clef. See also *bass clef; treble clef.*

middle C

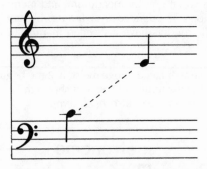

middle pedal   a pedal on the piano, also called the sostenuto (sustained) pedal. When depressed, the key or keys just sounded will be sustained. Subsequently depressed keys will not. See also *piano; sostenuto.*

military drum   an indefinite pitch drum slightly larger than the snare drum. See also *drum; percussion family.*

mineur   (Fr.) minor (key).

minim   the English name for the half note, derived from the mensural term, minima. See also *half note; mensural music.*

minim

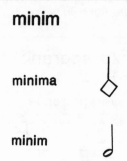

minima

minim

minor interval   an interval in which the upper note of a major interval has been reduced one half step. This is possible on intervals of the 2nd, 3rd, 6th and 7th degrees. When upper notes of the perfect 4th, 5th, and 8th (octave) are reduced, the result is a diminished interval. See also *interval; major interval;* and **Scales, Keys and Chords.**

---

minor interval

---

minor scale

flats when
descending

---

minor scale   a scale modifying the intervals of the related major scales. The key signature for a minor scale is identical to that of the major scale one and one-half steps above. Example: Both C minor and E flat major have the time signature of three flats. And both E minor and G major have a key signature of one sharp.

When notes are sounded in accordance with the key signature, the scale is called the natural minor. More common, though, is the harmonic minor, in which the 7th degree (the leading tone) is raised one half step. A third form, the melodic minor, involves a raised 6th and 7th degrees when ascending, and a return to pitch indicated by the key signature when descending. See also *harmonic minor scale; melodic minor scale; natural minor scale;* and **Scales, Keys and Chords.** See illustration, page 129.

minore (It.) minor (key).

minstrel (1) a medieval singer or performer, also called a troubadour. (2) 19th and 20th century black-face singers, a form of entertainment popular in the United States. See also *song; troubadour; vocal music.*

minuet a 17th and 18th century dance of French origin, written in triple time and performed in moderate tempo. As instrumental music, the minuet gained acceptance as a movement in the suite and as the third movement of symphonies and string quartets. See also *dance; sonata form; suite.*

mirror canon a canon with parts performed simultaneously, but written exactly opposite of one another. When notes in one part ascend, notes in the mirror part descend. See also *canon; inversion.*

mirror canon

mirror fugue a fugue with inverted forms of the same theme. Ascending themes are subjected to fugue treatment, and also are performed in descending form. See also *fugue; inversion.* See illustration, page 131.

mixed voices a choir or other vocal group, comprised of both male and female voices. See also *choir; vocal music.*

Mixolydian mode a Church mode of all natural tones beginning and ending on the note G. See also *Church modes; mode.* See illustration, page 131.

modality descriptive of music composed in one of the Church modes, in comparison to the modern use of major and minor diatonic formations. See also *Church modes; neomodal; tonality.*

mirror fugue

Mixolydian mode

mode **(1)** the intervals of a scale, strictly applied regardless of the key. Example: the diatonic major mode consists of whole tones between each degree except degrees 3 to 4, and 7 to 8, which are half tones. **(2)** antiquated Church modes that are represented by natural tones beginning and ending on various pitches. **(3)** a pattern (rhythmic mode) used in the 13th century, identifying combinations of rhythm in 3/4 meter. See also *Church modes; diatonic; pentatonic scale; rhythmic mode; scale.*

moderato   (It.) moderately.

modern dance   ballet and other forms of dance in stage performance, as practiced in the 20th century. See also *ballet; dance.*

Modern period   the period of music beginning approximately in 1900, and immediately following the period of Romantic music. Modern music is notably contrasted with Romantic style in the use of dissonance, experimentation with now chordal variety, and atonality. The mathematical certainty of four-measure phrasing found in music of the past is not in style during the Modern period. Frequent changes in time signature and the use of complicated meter are common. Trends in the twelve-tone system and the use of electronic music are significant developments in the Modern period. See also *atonal music; dissonance; Romantic music; twelve-tone music.*

modulation   the orderly change from one key to another, in such a manner that the change is not abrupt or distracting to the listener. This is achieved by the introduction of a common chord, that directly or through a progression of other chords, resolves to the tonic in the second key. Modulation is simple when moving to a key separated from the first key by few changes in key signature (separated by differences of one or two accidentals only). Example: To modulate from the key of G major to C major, the G (tonic) chord is followed by a D (dominant) chord, then a G7 (the dominant in the key of C), and then a C major chord (the new tonic). See also *common chord; key; pivot chord; tonality; transition.*

modulation

moll   (G.) minor (key).

moment   **(1)** a short segment in a composition that possesses characteristics apart from the nature of the movement of composition as a whole; a departure in texture, key, volume or tempo. **(2)** name assigned to each section of a suite, a theme and variations, or other composition containing relatively short segments. See also *composition; suite; theme and variations.*

monocordo   (It.) play on one string.

monody   (1) "single song," a melody that is accompanied by chords or a single bass line. In this form, the monodic theme is of primary importance, and accompaniment is secondary. (2) a song for one singer. See also *continuo; melody; song; vocal music.*

monophonic sound   one sound, a melody without accompaniment. See also *folk music; homophonic sound; melody; polyphony.*

monothematic   a composition based on a single melody or theme. See also *fugue; melody; theme.*

monotone   (1) the singing of a phrase on a single note, often a practice in segments of liturgical music. (2) a person who cannot sing the correct pitch, or who is unable to match a sounded note. See also *chant; Gregorian chant; liturgical music; pitch.*

morbido   (It.) smoothly, gently.

mordent   a short trill from the written note to the note immediately above. (An inverted mordent involves the written note and the one immediately below.) The length of the mordent depends on the tempo and time value of the note. This form of notation today is often replaced with ornaments written in, or replaced by the trill. See also *inverted mordent; notation; ornament; trill.*

---

mordent

---

morendo   (It.) fading away.

mosso   (It.) animated.

motet   (1) a vocal composition in medieval music, in which established melody and words were combined with polyphonic variations, and with new harmonies or melodies. This form, in use from the 13th and 14th centuries, included three vocal parts. (2) a form in use during the 15th and 16th centuries, also called the Flemish motet, with either four or five vocal parts and written in polyphonic form. (3) liturgical vocal music in the Roman Catholic service, similar to the anthem in the Anglican service. See also *anthem; choral; liturgical music; polyphony; Renaissance music; vocal music.*

motion **(1)** the pattern of movement in a single part or voice, either ascending or descending. **(2)** the pattern of relative movement in two separate parts or voices, including: *similar motion*—two parts moving up or down at the same time, but not maintaining the same interval; *parallel motion*—similar motion, but with the same interval maintained; *contrary motion*—two parts moving in opposite directions; *oblique motion*—one part remaining on the same note, while the other changes. See also *conjunct; contrary motion; line; movement; oblique motion; parallel motion; similar motion.*

motion

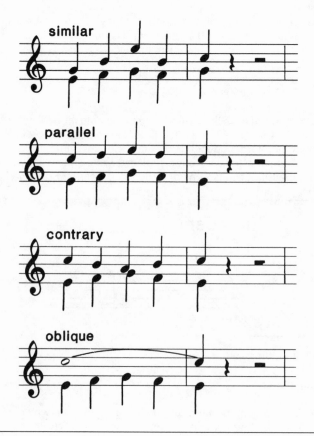

motive (motif) **(1)** a recognizable, combined rhythmic and melodic pattern, which runs through a movement or several movements of one composition. **(2)** vague reference to the leading motif. See also *leading motif; leitmotiv; theme.*

moto (It.) motion.

motto   a theme that is stated and, later in the same composition, recalled or repeated. See also *theme*.

mouthpiece   part of a wind instrument that connects with the player's lips. There are three types: the single reed (clarinets, saxophones), the double reed (oboe), and the mouth hole (flute). See also *reed; wind family*.

movement   **(1)** the distinct sections of a larger work, such as the movements of a concerto, symphony, suite or string quartet. Each movement in a single composition may be distinguished in terms of style, key and tempo. Yet, the combined movements represent a single composition. **(2)** descriptive of the vertical makeup of a composition, or the combined melody and rhythm; or of the horizontal features in music, consisting of harmony. **(3)** descriptive of the pattern of motion in a single part or voice, or of relative motions in two or more parts. See also *concerto; motion; sonata form; string quartet; suite; symphony*.

muffle   covering a drum with a cloth to create a muted effect. See also *drum; mute*.

multi-tonal   descriptive of a composition in which the key changes frequently, popular from the late 19th century through the Modern period. See also *bitonality; tonality*.

mundharmonika   (G.) see *harmonica*.

music drama   a form of opera popularized by Wagner, in which the orchestra is more prominent than the vocal parts. Music is sounded continuously in each act. Characters, themes and emotions are suggested and repeated by a leitmotiv for each. See also *leitmotiv; opera; vocal music*.

musica ficta   (Lt.) "false music," the practice of adding accidentals that were not written in by the composer. Vocal music written up to the 16th century, in modes lacking leading tones, was unnatural to sing as written. Increasing the leading tone by a half step was a natural and logical practice. In modern scores of music written in the past, musica ficta is indicated by writing assumed placement of accidentals above the note. Example: In the Dorian mode, the final (tonic) is D. When singing the written note C, it is logical to increase the pitch to C sharp. See also *accidental; leading tone; vocal music*.

---

musica ficta

musical comedy   a stage play that may include musical, spoken and dance segments. Vocal music is most often for one or two voices, although multiples above that are not unusual. The musical comedy is less structured than the operetta. See also *dance; operetta; vocal music.*

musical period

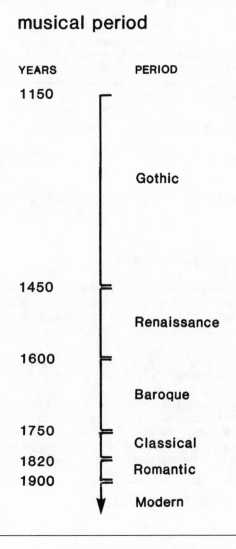

YEARS	PERIOD
1150	
	Gothic
1450	
	Renaissance
1600	
	Baroque
1750	
	Classical
1820	Romantic
1900	
	Modern

musical period   names assigned to ranges of years, in which music underwent transitions and new ideas were introduced and developed. A distinction must be made between actual major periods and transitional practices. Example: The impressionistic and expressionistic theories occurred at the end of the Romantic period, and were named for trends taking place in other arts. The names were adopted to describe specific attitudes about musical composition. However, they were not actual musical periods in the strict sense. They were temporary and experimental times, represented by the music being written by a few major composers of the day.

The beginning and ending dates of major musical periods are assigned based on the prominence of major composers. In reality, changes in style, practice, and attitude are very gradual. Periods actually overlap and cannot be strictly said to start and stop on certain dates. In historical perspective, what is today called the Modern period might be assigned a different name, and its total length cannot be known until newer trends develop and come into popular use. See also *Baroque; classical; Gothic period; Modern period; Renaissance music; Romantic music.* See illustration, page 136.

musical saw   a hand-saw played with a violin bow. By bending the saw and changing the degree of tension with the left hand, while bowing with the right, pitch can be changed. See also *bow; pitch.*

musicology   the scholarly examination of music, including research of sources and developments, composition style, and social influences on compositon and performance. See also *composition.*

musikalische säge   (G.) see *musical saw.*

mutation   (1) the transition from one hexachord to another. (2) a stop on the organ. When in use, a harmonic of the depressed note is sounded, rather than the note itself. (3) the change in a male voice, occurring at the onset of puberty. See also *harmonics; hexachord; organ; stop; transition; voice.*

mute   a device that muffles or softens the sound of an instrument, similar to a damper, which lowers or eliminates a sound. Mutes include the piano's soft pedal, the clamp-like device used on string instruments, the wooden mute used on brass instruments, the muffle that covers a drum, and the soft-headed drumstick. See also *damper; muffle; soft pedal.*

N

naked fifth   see *open fifth.*

nationalism   music that, by its character, is associated with a particular country. This trait, a feature often found in Romantic music, results from the use of rhythms, melodic patterns, instrumentation or basing melodies on folk music. Notable nationalistic composers inlcude Chopin, Grieg, Dvorak, Copland, Moussorgsky, and Rimsky-Korsakoff, among others. See also *folk music; Romantic music.*

natural **(1)** a note that is neither sharp nor flat, represented by the white keys on the piano. **(2)** a brass instrument that is played without the use of valves or keys, capable of playing only those tones in a harmonic series. **(3)** a natural harmonic, produced by touching rather than depressing an open string. See also *accidental; flat; harmonic series; sharp.*

natural

natural minor scale a variation of the minor scale in which the third, sixth, and seventh degrees are flattened. Example: In the key of C minor, the natural minor scale is C, D, E-flat, F, G, A-flat, B-flat, and C. See also *harmonic minor scale; melodic minor scale; minor scale;* and **Scales, Keys and Chords.**

natural tone see *open note.*

naturale (It.) natural; instruction to return to natural performance, from a deviated form, such as falsetto (voice) or muted (instrument). See also *falsetto; mute.*

naturel (Fr.) see *natural.*

natürlich (G.) see *natural.*

Neapolitan sixth a chord appearing in the music of the 18th century, consisting of a flattened supertonic. In the key of C, for example, the chord, is made up of F, A flat, and D flat. See also *chord; sixth; supertonic.*

Neopolitan sixth

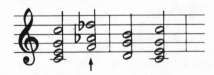

neck the section of a stringed instrument containing the finger board. See also *finger board; string family.*

neighboring tone   a note that is sounded but is not a part of the chord structure itself; an ornament. These are a half step above or below the chord's legitimate note. The chord's tone is sounded, followed by the neighboring tone, then a return to the chord's tone. Example: An upper neighboring tone occurs in the progression of E-F-E, while a C major chord is sounded. Example: A lower neighboring tone occurs in the progression G-F#-G, while a G chord is sounded. See also *auxiliary tone; nonharmonic tone; ornament.*

neighboring tone

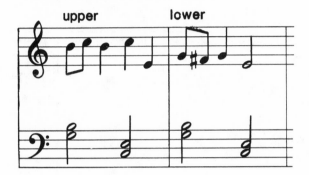

neoclassicism   a movement in 20th century music, that rejected the emotional character found in Romantic music. Forms of composition practices in past musical periods were again popularized, albeit in combination with trends toward dissonance and greater freedom of rhythmic complexities. See also *Modern period; Romantic music.*

neomodal   descriptive of 20th century music that makes use of, or imitates the Church modes. See also *Church modes; mode.*

neoromanticism   the latter part of the Romantic period, from approximately 1880 through 1910. The term also is applied to the trend in Modern music away from neoclassicism. See also *Modern period; Romantic music.*

neumes   shorthand forms of musical notation used before development of modern-day rounded notes, stems, five-line staffs, and measures. Neumes date from as early as the 9th century, when plainsong notation for single tones and small clusters was written without the use of staffs. These earlier symbols were intended only as general guidelines to singers as to a line's direction, rather than specific pitches. These are referred to as cheironomic (hand-sign) neumes.

  With the development of a four-line staff, a new form of neumes came into use, called heightened, or intervallic. Replacing the vague line and dot indicators were squared notes and stems. This form of notation is referred to generally as ligature, due to the tendency to tie clusters of notes together in a string of neumes. For the first time, notes gave not only precise pitch, but also rhythmic value. Still, the exact duration of neumes varied from one use to another.

A transition between neumes and modern notation is found in the mensural notation formulated during the 13th century. With this system, notes had both pitch and time value, although actual measure lines did not come into popular use until as late as the 17th century. See also *Gregorian chant; ligature; measure; mensural music; notation systems; plainsong; staff.*

neumes

CHEIRONOMIC	INTERVALLIC	MODERN
punctum		
virga		
podatus		
clivis		
climacus		
porrectus		
scandicus		
torculus		

nicht gestopft (G.) not stopped (horn notation).

ninth (1) an interval of nine steps, or the combination of an octave and a second. (2) also called the dominant 9th, a 7th chord with the added 9th degree.

Example: In the key of C, the ninth is made up of the notes C, E, G, B and D. See also *chord; interval.*

---

ninth

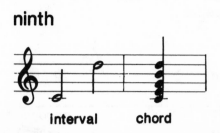

interval   chord

---

nocturne **(1)** night piece, an 18th and 19th century composition for several instruments. **(2)** a short, romantic or lyrical composition for the piano. **(3)** name assigned to a movement in a larger work, to imply a romantic or gentle quality. See also *character piece; piano; serenade.*

non tanto (It.) not as much.

non troppo (It.) not too much.

nonet chamber music composed for nine instruments. See also *chamber music; ensemble.*

non-functional harmony progressions of chords that do not lead to natural resolutions or finals, added only to supply sound or fill in parts; lacking the harmonic progression associated with harmonic purpose. See also *chord; functional harmony; harmony; progression; resolution.*

nonharmonic tone a tone that embellishes and adds flavor or variety to music, but is not a part of the chord being sounded at the moment.

Every nonharmonic tone can be described by (a) the method of approach, or the origination of the tone in relation to the harmonic tone; (b) the method of quitting, or resolution from nonharmonic to harmonic tone; and (c) the way that the tone is quitted (by resolution toward or away from the direction of music, or by holding the tone until a subsequent chord is sounded).

Nonharmonic tones are either rhythmically weak or strong. A weak tone occurs in between other notes that are themselves part of the harmony. Strong tones occur in place of the harmonic tone.

Rhythmically weak nonharmonic tones include anticipation, auxiliary tone, cambiata tone, échappée and passing tone. Rhythmically strong nonharmonic tones include appoggiatura and suspension.

anticipation—a note sounded immediately in advance of the chord to which it belongs.

auxiliary tone—a note that departs from the harmonic chord, usually by a half step, and immediately returns.

nonharmonic tone

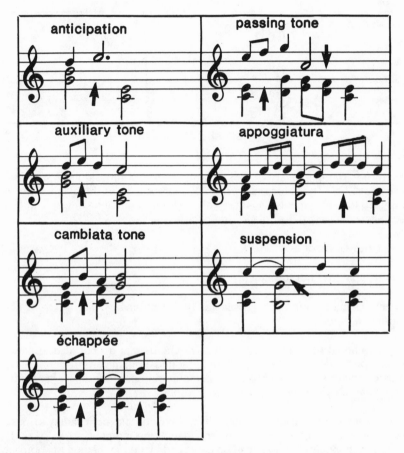

cambiata tone—a departure from a chord by way of a leap, quitted with a single step in the opposite direction. For example, while the C chord is being sounded, the top voice sounds G, then the cambiata B, followed by an A as part of the next chord, F major.

échappée—a tone departing from the harmonic chord and quitted by a leap in the opposite direction.

passing tone—a tone or series of tones appearing as connections between harmonic chords, approached from and quitted to harmonic tones, usually without leaps.

appoggiatura—a leap away from the harmonic chord, with multiple nonharmonic tones sounded before resolution, or an extended series of grace notes. Approach is usually by way of a leap, and the tone or series of tones are quitted most often by a step. (Note: the appoggiatura has a second meaning, as a simple ornament written immediately before its subject note, and having no time value. This is indicated with a small note and a slash through its stem.)

suspension—a note held over from a harmonic chord, becomes nonharmonic as a subsequent chord is sounded, and then resolves by changing to another tone. Example: The top voice sounds an F over an F chord. The note is held while a C major chord sounds, and then resolves to the harmonic E.

See also *anticipation; appoggiatura; auxiliary tone; cambiata tones; échappée; neighboring tone; ornament; passing tone; suspension.* See illustration, page 142.

non-transposing instrument   any instrument that sounds pitches identical to those written. Many instruments transpose above or below the written note, a practice that avoids excessive use of ledger lines when an instrument's range does not conform to the staff range. Non-transposing instruments have ranges within the general scope of the staff. Orchestral non-transposing instruments include the flute, oboe, bassoon, trombone, tuba, piano, tympani, violin, viola and cello. See also *transposing instrument.*

notation   the symbols, instructions and codes used in various forms of music to instruct performers as to the method and nuance of play. Forms of notation include:

a. tempo—the speed of performance, which is indicated by written words above the staff. Italian tempo names—such as allegro, adagio, andante, and largo—are in universal use, although instructions in English and other languages are acceptable as well.

b. volume—the degree of loudness. The abbreviation "f" indicates forte (loud), and "p" indicates piano (soft). Changes in volume are indicated by forks, from loud to soft or soft to loud.

c. meter—the time signature of music. The signature consists of two numbers, such as 3/4. The upper number is the number of beats per measure, and the lower number tells the type of note (half, quarter, etc.).

d. rhythm—the duration value of notes or rests within a measure; or with ties, over two or more measures. Note values are divided into whole, half, quarter, eighth, sixteenth, and smaller values. It is possible to notate irregular groupings (triplets, doublets, etc.). Note values are extended with dots and ties.

e. pitch—the placement of a circular note on a line or space within the staff or, with ledger lines, above or below the staff. The system in use today is the result of hundreds of years of evolution in notation systems (see next entry).

f. special instructions—performance techniques or methods, including repeat, trill, mordent, pizzacato, mute, glissando, and other departures from the usual method of playing notes or producing sounds.

g. key signature—the number of sharps or flats in effect, shown at the left of each line of music after the staff identification. Any departure from the key signature in effect is notated by placing accidentals in front of the note to be sounded.

h. abbreviated forms—any notation that substitutes the written-out note or chord. Included are chord names. The chord's name (C, G7, Dm, etc.) is written above the line, but the inversion of the chord is not stated. Thus, a "C" can consist of C-E-G, E-G-C, or G-C-E. Another abbreviated form is the chord symbols, as used in guitar music. The figured bass is another abbreviated form, a system

notation

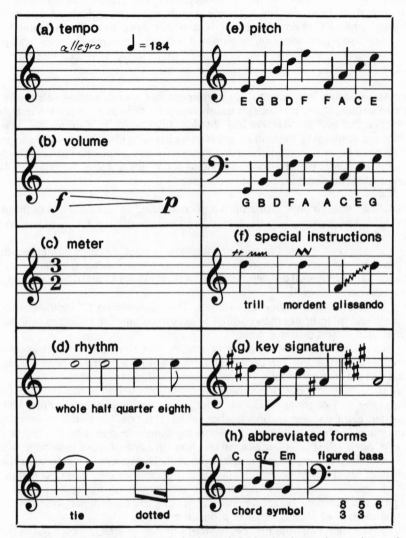

(a) tempo
allegro ♩ = 184

(b) volume
f ———————— *p*

(c) meter
3/2

(d) rhythm
whole half quarter eighth

tie   dotted

(e) pitch
E G B D F   F A C E

G B D F A   A C E G

(f) special instructions
trill   mordent glissando

(g) key signature

(h) abbreviated forms
C G7 Em   figured bass

chord symbol   8 5 6
                3 3

of coded symbols written beneath the bass clef. This let the performer know the appropriate chord and inversion, but left room for improvisation.

See also *accidental; chord symbol; figured bass; irregular grouping; key signature; meter; pitch; rhythm; tempo; time signature; volume;* **Illustrated Notation Guide;** and **Scales, Keys and Chords.**

notation systems   coded methods of writing notes and performance directions, including:

notation systems

notation systems

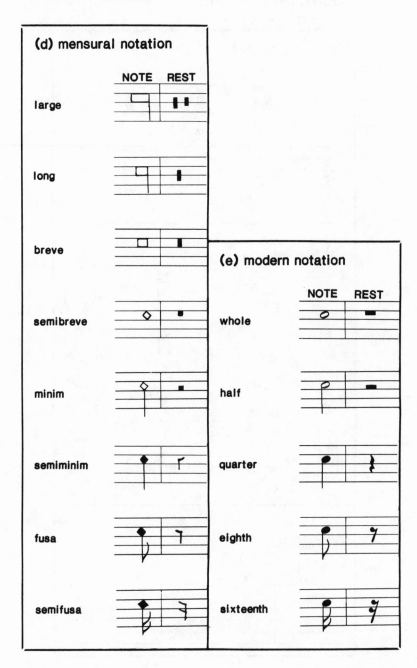

a. chord symbols—common in guitar music scores and scores of popular music. In addition to a melody line (and usually, actual bass harmony line), the symbol is written above the line. Symbols may be limited to the name alone—C, Em, G7, etc.—but more often also include the guitar chord grid. A chord symbol by itself leaves it to the performer to select the method of playing the chord.

b. neumes—plainsong notation also called ligature, in use from the 9th to 11th centuries. Ascending and descending notes were joined together in limited combinations. However, without measures, the exact rhythm value of notes was not included.

c. tablature—a shorthand system of the 16th and 17th centuries, for the lute and other stringed instruments. Notes were written on six-line staffs, each line representing a string of the instrument. Letters or numbers were written in spaces to instruct the performer as to which strings to stop, and on which frets.

d. mensural notation—developed in the 13th century and preceding modern notation. Duration values of notes were developed, although consistency from one use to another was not possible without the use of distinct measures.

e. modern notation—notes now are rounded, and duration values are consistent. The most significant development in modern notation is the addition of measures, separated by bar lines. Time values greater than whole notes are not in use, and extended sounded pitches are notated with ties.

See also *chord symbol; ligature; mensural notation; neumes; tablature.* See illustrations, pages 145, 146.

note   the written symbol for each pitch, named alphabetically from A to G, or by equivalent names in the solmization system. See also *fasola; pitch; solmization; tone.*

---

note

doh ray mi fah sol lah ti doh

---

nuance   a variation in tempo or phrasing of music. See also *phrasing; tempo.*

nut   (1) a ridge on which strings pass above the finger board of a violin, viola, cello or double bass. (2) the handle of a stringed instrument's bow. (3) a capo, used on the guitar or other stringed instrument to eliminate one or more frets, to enable players to easily transpose into new keys. See also *bow; capo; finger board; string family.*

O

obbligato (It.) **(1)** an accompaniment or section of music that is optional. It may be either played or omitted. **(2)** In its original meaning, the opposite of the first definition: an essential section of music. See also *accompaniment*.

oblique motion relative motion in two voices, in which one part sounds a single note, and the other changes. See also *motion*.

oblique motion

oboe an end-blown, conical-bore woodwind instrument played with a double reed. The oboe is a standard orchestral instrument, is used in military bands and chamber music, and is suited for solo parts. Its natural scale is in D and its range extends over 2½ octaves. See also *double reed; reed; wind family*.

oboe

oboe family instruments commonly developed from the medieval shawm, including the English horn, bassoon, and contrabassoon. Less common instruments in the oboe family are the E flat oboe, oboe d'amore, heckelphone, and oboe da caccia. See also *woodwind*.

octave a perfect interval of 12 half steps, or eight diatonic steps. Example: The A to the next highest A, or B to B, or C to C, are octaves. This interval can be diminished (lowered one half step) or augmented (raised one half step). See also *interval; perfect interval*. See illustration, page 149.

octet an ensemble of eight instruments or voices, or as composition for eight performers (often a double quartet). See also *ensemble; quartet*.

octave

---

ode **(1)** a song or other composition of praise. **(2)** a musical version of a poem, often of a religious nature. **(3)** a free-form composition including orchestra, chorus and soloists. See also *anthem; song; vocal music.*

offen (G.) open.

one-line instrument any instrument whose notation is written on a single staff. In comparison, certain instruments (piano, organ, and xylophone, for example) require a double staff. See also *instrumentation; staff.*

one-movement symphony a symphony that contains one movement rather than the more common three of four. The single movement usually is longer than the typical movement, and may develop to the point that it has the same degree of variety as multi-movement compositions. See also *symphony.*

open not stopped; a string played without depressing, for example. See also *stopped.*

open fifth a chord in which the first and fifth degrees are sounded, but the third degree (mediant) is not. Its sound is hollow, and the absense of the third degree is apparent, and is considered an undesirable chord formation. See also *chord; interval; triad.*

---

open fifth

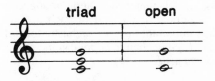

---

open harmony a formation of chords that span a distance greater than a single octave. See also *chord; close harmony; harmony; octave; position.* See illustration, page 150.

open note a note played on brass or wind instruments without depressing keys or valves, also called a natural tone; on string instruments, notes sounded on open strings. See also *natural; open; stopped.*

open harmony

open score a score with one line for each instrument in the ensemble. See also *condensed score; ensemble; orchestral score; score.*

open string a string played without being depressed. See also *fingering; open; stopped.*

open tone see *open note.*

opera (It.) from "opera in musica," or work in music, a combination vocal and orchestral dramatic work. It originated in Italy at the beginning of the 17th century. Some operas contain spoken parts with musical background (melodrama), although in most operas, all vocal parts are sung.

In the 17th and 18th centuries, rigid style and format were the rule, and greater prominence was given to virtuosity of individual singers, than to the musical score or dramatic value of the performance. Wagner's later operas, also called music dramas, placed greater value and importance on the music, which sounded from the beginning to the end of each act, without pause. Vocal segments became less important than the orchestra toward the end of the 19th century. See also *ballad opera; chamber opera; grand opera; melodrama; music drama; operetta; vocal music.*

opera ballet a form of musical stage production in which ballet and opera forms are combined. See also *ballet.*

opéra bouffe (Fr.) see *comic opera.*

opera buffa (It.) see *comic opera.*

opéra comique (Fr.) **(1)** an 18th century comic opera with spoken parts in addition to singing. **(2)** a 19th century operatic form, describing any opera containing spoken parts, whether comical or serious. See also *comic opera*.

opera seria (It.) a serious opera, as opposed to a comic opera. During the 18th century, an opera seria had an epic or heroic theme and plot, an Italian libretto, and was highly formalized. See also *comic opera; libretto*.

operetta (It.) "little opera," a stage performance with music, spoken parts, and dance. The term describes musical comedies as well as presentations with sung dialogue. An operetta is generally more closely associated with opera than with musical comedy. See also *dance; musical comedy; vocal music*.

opposite mode the minor mode related to the major mode of the same name (C minor and C major), or the opposite—the major equivalent of a minor mode. See also *key; mode*. See illustration, page 152.

opposite motion relative motion in two voices or parts, in which the direction of a line is directly opposite that of another. See also *motion*. See illustration, page 153.

opus (It.) work; the numerical identification assigned to a composition or series of compositions by a composer. See also *composition*.

oratorio a musical form originated at the beginning of the 17th century, specifically for the expression of religious ideals or worship. It contains chorus and soloists, and orchestral parts. See also *liturgical music; vocal music*.

orchestra "dancing place," from the Greek phrase describing an arched section in front of the stage, where the chorus of a Greek play is situated. The modern orchestra is an organized ensemble of instruments, originating as part of the opera in the early 17th century. The symphony orchestra of today evolved from the chamber and string orchestras of the past, and contains four major sections: woodwinds, brass, percussion and strings.

A full ensemble may contain many specialized instruments in addition to the usual complement. Below is a typical standard orchestra:

woodwinds	*brass*
1	piccolo
3	flute
2−3	oboe
1	English horn
2−3	clarinet
1	bass clarinet
2−3	bassoon
1	contrabassoon
4−8	horn
3−5	trumpet
3−4	trombone
1	tuba

opposite mode

opposite motion

percussion		strings	
3−4	tympani	14−18	1st violin
1	cymbal	14−16	2nd violin
1	tenor drum	12	viola
1	bass drum	10−12	cello
		8	double bass

See also *brass family; percussion family; string family; wind family.*

orchestral score   the complete score, with all instrumental parts and (if applicable) soloists and vocal parts, written out in full. It is used by the conductor. Individual players have only their own parts before them. See also *conduct; open score; score.*

orchestration   the selection of instruments and combination of sounds, to achieve the desired tonal effect. The composer must be aware of performance potential and limitations for each instrument; its best ranges; degree of power and mix with other sounds, for control of dynamics and tonal quality; and the ability to play certain pitches or progressions on an instrument. See also *arrangement; score.*

organ   a keyboard instrument with several manual keyboards and foot pedals. Wind is forced under pressure through a series of pipes. In the past, this was done by way of a manually operated bellows. In most modern organs, air pressure is achieved electronically.
    Parts of the organ include:
    manual keyboards—numbering from one to five (or more), with three to four keyboards most common. The first two are called the swell organ (upper) and great organ (lower). A third manual is called the choir organ. If a fourth keyboard is present, it assumes the top position, and is given the name solo organ.
    pedal board—an additional keyboard, played with the feet. It contains the same mixture and arrangement of notes—white and black keys—as other keyboards of the organ.
    couplers—these enable the player to transfer the stops available on one manual to another. For example, the coupler labeled "swell to great" transfers

organ

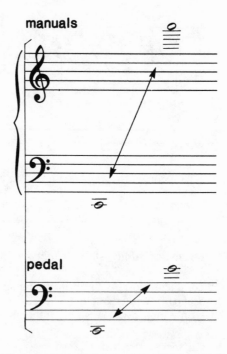

---

all stops on the swell manual over to the great. Any manual can also be coupled to the pedal, and the pedal to any manual.

stops — groupings of controls that activate various pipes or pipe groups with a particular tone color, associated with the various orchestral instruments. By drawing a stop, the performer brings into action that series of tones. The combination of stops in use at any moment makes up the total quality of sound produced by depressing keys.

Performers control and expand sound by activating stops. Certain stop combinations can be pre-arranged and then brought into play with a single switch. Range of play can also be expanded with the use of stops other than the 8-foot variety (which play the exact pitch played). For example, a 4-foot stop sounds an octave higher than the note played, and a 2-foot stop sounds two octaves higher. Octaves can be lowered in similar fashion by activating 16- and 32-foot stops.

Besides the foundation stops described above, organs contain mutation stops, which reinforce overtones. These are given whole and fractional number names, identifying specific overtones they emphasize. When stops combine foundation and mutation features, they are referred to as mixture stops. These add the greatest enrichment to total sound of all stops on the organ.

Stops are classified in four groups. String stops are sharp and clear, although not necessarily of the same tonal quality as the string instruments. Flute stops correspond to orchestral woodwind instruments. Diapason stops add foundation to the combined use of other stops. By themselves, they have little color; in use with other sounds, they round out the quality of overall texture. Reed stops represent the brass instruments of the orchestra.

pipes—actual pipes of various sizes and constructed from different materials, or imitated sounds of pipes produced electronically.

See also *electronic instrument; keyboard instrument; manual keyboard; pedal; pipe; registration; stop.* See illustration, page 154.

organetto   (It.) see *harmonium.*

organo   (It.) (Sp.) see *organ.*

organum   the early development of polyphony, that first appeared in the 9th century. A second voice was introduced in Gregorian chants, by one of four techniques:

a. strict—also called parallel organum, this evolved between the 9th and 12th centuries. It consists of parallel fourths and fifths, with harmony appearing in the lower voice. Motion is strictly parallel (either from beginning to end, or as a departure from a chant beginning in unison). The harmonized part probably was sung by a soloist, while the balance of the choir sang the primary line in unison.

b. free—11th and 12th century form derived from strict organum, a variation in which the lower, harmonizing voice varied from parallel intervals. Either a single note was held while the upper voice changed, or the interval itself was adjusted. The lower voice did not extend below the note C (below middle C), probably as a matter of voice range. In addition, certain intervals were impractical for vocal performance. Thus, different tones were introduced in replacement, resulting in intervals of the second, third or sixth; or in variations between perfect fourths and fifths.

c. new—also called measured organum, this came into use in the 11th and 12th centuries. It is characterized by strict triple meter and contrary motion (two parts moving in opposing directions). The preference was for variety in motion, combining parallel, oblique, and contrary. Voices were also allowed to cross, and the lower voice was considered the primary one.

d. melismatic—developed in the 12th century, the lower voice sang the primary part in long notes. The upper voice sang a varied, often elaborate counter-melody. This part may have been improvised, and the form probably was reserved for specific segments of music, rather than carried through an entire chant. The upper part (called duplum) contained up to 10 notes, against a single note in the lower (called tenor) voice.

See also *contrary motion; Gregorian chant; harmony; interval; motion; oblique motion; parallel motion; plainsong; polyphony; vocal music.* See illustration, page 156.

orgel   (G.) see *organ.*

orgue   (Fr.) see *organ.*

organum

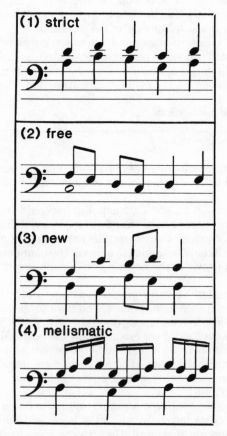

ornament   nonharmonic notes in instrumental music added for flavor and variety; or alterations in the methods of playing specific notes. The trill is common in 19th and 20th century music, while other forms were more popular during earlier periods. See also *arpeggio; embellishment; grace note; mordent; nonharmonic tone; trill; turn;* and **Illustrated Notation Guide.**

ornamentation   the method of notating ornaments, through (a) symbols or abbreviations; (b) writing out additional notes; or (c) writing instructions above the line. See also **Illustrated Notation Guide.**

ostinato   (It.) a repeated phrase, melodic section or rhythmic pattern. It recurs throughout a composition, often in the same part (frequently in the bass). See also *phrase.*

ottava   (It.) octave; a sign, abbreviated *8va,* instructing the instrumentalist to play notes exactly one octave higher than as written. The phrase ottava bassa (or, *8va bassa*) tells the performer to play one octave lower then as written. See also *octave*.

ottava

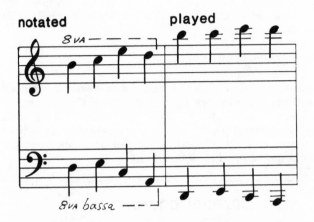

outer voices   descriptive of the top and bottom parts in vocal music. In a four-part vocal composition, the soprano (top voice) and bass (bottom voice) are outer; the alto and tenor are inner. See also *inner voices; vocal music.*

ouvert   (Fr.) opening; instruction to play the first of two cadences.

overblowing   a technique for woodwind instruments, in which the lips and breath are used in such a way that higher range notes are sounded with lower range fingering. Overblowing produces pitch exactly one octave above as fingered, except on the clarinet, when a twelfth results. See also *embouchure; woodwind.*

overtone   **(1)** see *open note.* **(2)** see *harmonic series.*

overture   **(1)** a strictly instrumental section preceding the first act of an opera, often based on themes occurring later in the production; or an introduction played before the opening act of a ballet. **(2)** a medley of themes played before the first act of a musical comedy. **(3)** a one-movement composition for orchestra that has a style similar to that of the operatic form. **(4)** instrumental introduction played before the beginning of a non-musical play. **(5)** obsolete definition of the suite. See also *ballet; medley; musical comedy; opera; suite.*

P

pandiatonicism   in 20th century music, a development away from atonal composition, toward use of the diatonic scale. Atonal music is the absence of a tonal center, whereas pandiatonic music is the recognition of one or more distinct diatonic keys. When multiple keys are in use, harmonies may occur in multiple keys at the same time. Example: One voice sounds a G major chord while another sounds a melody in the key of D major. See also *atonal music; diatonic; Modern period; neoclassicism.*

parade drum   see *military drum.*

parallel chords   chords that progress upward or downward without a change in their structures. The root triad containing degrees (from bottom to top) one, three and five are not desirable in parallel chords, due to the resulting parallel fifths. If the avoidance of parallel perfect intervals is to be respected in parallel chords, intervals of the fourth and octave will be avoided as well. See also *chord; faux bourdon; parallel motion; triad.*

---

parallel chords

---

parallel fifths   the progression of two separate voices or parts, in the same direction and to the same degree. Moving from one chord to another produces two or more consecutive intervals of the perfect fifth. Until the beginning of the 20th century, parallel fifths were considered undesirable. See also *consecutive interval; fifth; harmony; hidden fifth; interval; similar motion.*

---

parallel fifths

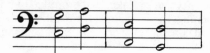

---

parallel key   two opposite modes; keys with the same name but not the same key signature. For example, the key of A major contains three sharps, while A minor has no sharps or flats. The minor parallel key signature for each major key is always identical to the key signature of the major key one and one-half steps above. See also *key; opposite mode; relative key.*

parallel motion   motion in which two parts move in the same direction and maintain the same interval. See also *consecutive interval; interval; motion; similar motion.*

---

parallel motion

---

parallel octave   the progression in two voices or parts, an octave apart. The perfect octave in parallel was not considered acceptable until the beginning of the 20th century. See also *consecutive interval; harmony; hidden octave; interval; octave; similar motion.*

---

parallel octave

---

paraphrase   the variation of an existing composition, such as a piano rendition of music written for orchestral performance. See also *variation.*

parlando   (It.) as if spoken.

part   **(1)** a voice or instrument in an ensemble for two or more performers. **(2)** a section of a composition, such as a movement in a symphony, sonata or suite. **(3)** one of the voices in a multiple-part contrapuntal composition, such as the first voice in a four-voice fugue.
   See also *contrapuntal; line; movement; voice.*

part music   descriptive of compositions with distinct lines or voices, as opposed to a single melody supported by harmony. See also *contrapuntal; line; madrigal.*

part song   a song written for several voices, with the soprano (highest voice) carrying the melody. The part song is also associated with chordal style rather than contrapuntal. See also *contrapuntal; melody; song; vocal music.*

part writing the combination of several voices or lines of music, with the purpose of creating a smooth and natural harmonic progression. See also *harmony; line; voice leading.*

partial the degrees of the harmonic series, which are assigned numbers in ascending order, beginning with the first (fundamental). See also *fundamental; harmonic series; overtone.*

passage (1) a section of music that is transitional or of minor importance. (2) term used to describe a section of music in which one instrument or voice plays a prominent part, such as a solo vocal passage in an otherwise instrumental score. See also *bridge; transition.*

passing tone a nonharmonic tone occurring in a discordant line between two harmonic tones. See also *auxiliary tone; harmony; nonharmonic tone.*

---

passing tone

---

passion liturgical music based on the story of the Crucifixion. Early examples (12th century) were in plainsong form, and later were composed as oratorios. See also *liturgical music; oratorio; plainsong.*

patter song a fast-paced, humorous song found in many operettas. See also *operetta; song; vocal music.*

pauke (G.) see *tympani.*

pause (1) see *fermata.* (2) see *rest.*

pedal (1) that part of an instrument operated by the feet. Pedals serve several different purposes. On the piano, pedals are used to sustain or to soften sound. On the organ, a full keyboard is played on the pedal. The harp's pedals alter the pitch of strings chromatically. And on the harpsichord, pedals are used as registers. (2) the fundamental tone in a harmonic series. See also *action; fundamental; harmonic series; harp; harpsichord; keyboard instrument; organ; piano; register.*

pedal harp alternate name of the traditional harp, with pedals for chromatic alteration of pitch. Another form, the chromatic harp, contains no pedals. See also *harp.*

pedal marks notation for the use of pedals on the piano. This notation is written beneath the staff, in one of three ways:

a. the abbreviation Ped., an instruction to depress the damper pedal. Release of the pedal is signalled by an asterick.

b. brackets, defining the duration for which the pedal is to remain depressed.

c. Continuous brackets in one of two versions: separate horizontal lines with vertical start and stop marks, or a continuous line with indented pauses. See also *keyboard instrument; notation; piano.*

---

pedal marks

written	brackets	continuous

pedal piano a piano used briefly in the 19th century, equipped with a pedal keyboard in addition to the manual keyboard. See also *keyboard instrument; piano.*

pedal point a long note held in the bass, while other parts change. See also *bass; oblique motion.*

---

pedal point

pedal tone **(1)** alternate name for pedal point. **(2)** a note repeated in the bass over several measures, while other parts change. **(3)** the lowest tone that can be sounded on a wind instrument. See also *bass; wind family.*

pedal tone

pedaling **(1)** the way a performer uses the pedals while playing the piano. **(2)** the method of playing the pedal keyboard on the organ, the equivalent of fingering on a manual keyboard.

See also *fingering; keyboard instrument; organ; piano.*

peg a pin on violins and other orchestral stringed instruments, located on the neck. Its purpose is to control or adjust the tension of the strings. See also *neck; string family.*

pentatonic scale a scale consisting of five tones in the octave. The best known version of this scale is represented by the black keys on the piano. See also *chromatic scale; diatonic; scale.*

pentatonic scale

percussion clef a clef used for indefinite pitch instruments. In place of a clef sign (treble, alto or bass), and ledger lines, a single line is used for indicating rhythms. This clef is used, for example, for drum music.

Another version of indefinite pitch is written on a five-line staff with a percussion clef—thick, double vertical lines. This clef is used for cymbal, triangle, gong and other percussion instruments (although the single-line version may also be used).

The five-line version is useful for percussion instruments that have high-low forms without definite pitch, such as the bongo.

Percussion instruments with definite pitch are written on the standard treble and bass clefs. See also *clef; indefinite pitch clef; rhythm;* and **Illustrated Notation Guide.**

---

percussion clef

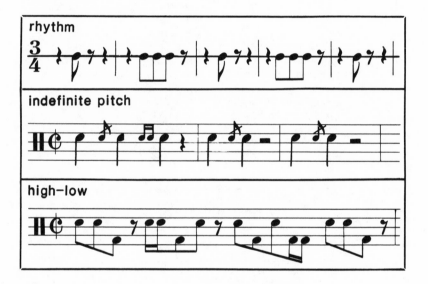

---

percussion family a large grouping of instruments, broken down into two categories:

a. definite pitch instruments, those struck or plucked to produce sound, and able to produce notes of definite pitch. Some have a limited capability (such as the tympani), while others are capable of sounding all notes within their range (such as all keyboard instruments). This group includes the entire family of keyboard instruments having strings that are struck or plucked. However, many consider the keyboard group as a distinct family of instruments separate from percussion.

b. indefinite pitch instruments, including the membranophone family (drums), and all instruments that are struck to produce rhythm and special effects.

The percussion family includes (but is not limited to):

definite pitch

celesta	chimes (bells)
clavichord	dulcimer
glockenspiel	harp
harpsichord	marimba
piano	spinet
tympani (timpani)	vibraphone
virginal	xylophone

indefinite pitch

bass drum	bongo
castanets	cymbal
gone (tam-tam)	log drum
maracas	military drum (parade drum)
musical saw	rattle
side drum	sleigh bells
slide whistle	snare drum
tambourine	tenor drum
tom-tom	triangle
whip	whistle
wood block (Chinese block, temple block)	

See also *drum; keyboard instrument; membranophone.*

perdendo   (It.) dying away.

perfect cadence

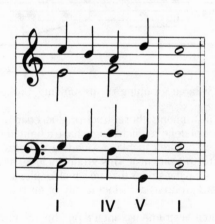

I   IV   V   I

perfect cadence   a progression of chords at the end of a section, phrase or movement, that contains the following characteristics:

(a) the final chord is the tonic;

(b) it is preceded by a chord of the fifth (dominant) or of the fourth (subdominant); and

(c) the root tone is in both the top and bottom positions of the final chord. See also *cadence; chord; imperfect cadence; progression.*

perfect interval   an interval of the fourth, fifth or octave (eighth), that is neither augmented nor diminished. See also *fifth; fourth; interval; just intonation; octave.*

---

perfect interval

---

perfect pitch   the ability, either held naturally or developed, to identify a pitch by sound alone. Relative pitch, in comparison, is the ability to identify intervals or to estimate a pitch's note value. See also *absolute pitch; pitch; relative pitch.*

period   **(1)** a musical statement, consisting of a number of measures with an easily identified beginning and end. **(2)** a range of years identified by specific characteristics of musical composition. See also *musical period; phrase.*

perpetual canon   descriptive of the form of a canon, when the last measure leads naturally to the first. Thus, the composition may be repeated indefinitely. See also *canon; phrase.*

pesante   (It.) heavily.

petite flûte   (Fr.) see *piccolo.*

pfeife   (G.) see *whistle.*

phrase   a musical statement, comparable to a sentence in a narrative. The four- and eight-measure phrase were traditional in Western music until the beginning of the 20th century. See also *period.*

phrasing   the method of performance of musical phrases. In written scores, the phrase is indicated by slurs, often added by editors at the time of publication. Wind and brass players must time breaths to correspond with natural phrases. And string players coordinate the direction of bowing in accordance with phrasing (except when, by notation, special effects are desired by special bowing techniques). See also *slur.* See illustration, page 166.

phrasing

Phrygian mode   a Church mode represented by the white keys on the piano, beginning and ending on the note E. See also *Church modes; mode.*

Phrygian mode

---

piacevole   (It.) pleasing.

pianissimo (pp)   (It.) very soft.

pianississimo (ppp)   (It.) extremely soft.

piano (p)   (It.) soft.

piano   popular name of the keyboard instrument pianoforte (It., "soft-loud"). The piano's strings are struck with hammers that are activated when keys are struck. The instrument was developed and came into popular use at the beginning of the 18th century. Bartolommeo Cristofori manufactured pianos in Florence, c. 1710, and named the instrument the *gravicembali col pian e forte* (the harpsichord with soft and loud by touch). The action that Christofori developed, consisting of a hammer hinged on a rail, is essentially the same device in use today.

The range of the piano extends seven octaves and a minor third. Its keyboard has 88 keys and either two or three foot pedals. On the right is the damper pedal which, when depressed, removes dampers from strings and allows them to continue vibrating after keys are released. The middle pedal, called the sostenuto, or sustaining pedal, is not found on all pianos. It enables the player to sustain tones for all keys depressed at the moment the pedal is activated. The pedal on the far left is called the soft pedal. By shifting the keys, fewer strings are struck by the hammer, reducing the volume.

The piano holds a notable advantage over the harpsichord. Performers are able to vary the volume, not just by use of the pedals, but by touch. A soft, delicate effect is possible, as well as a dramatic, deep volume. These effects, and other volumes in between, all are produced by the degree of power applied to the keys. See also *action; damper; grand piano; keyboard instrument; manual keyboard; soft pedal; sostenuto; spinet; sustain pedal; upright piano.*

piano

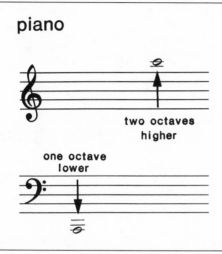

piano quartet **(1)** music written for an ensemble of violin, viola, cello and piano. **(2)** music written for performance by four pianos. See also *ensemble; quartet.*

piano quintet music written for an ensemble of two violins, viola, cello and piano; a string quartet plus a piano. See also *ensemble; quintet; string quartet.*

piano trio **(1)** music written for an ensemble of two string instruments and piano. The usual strings are violin and cello, or violin and viola. **(2)** music written for performance by three pianos. See also *ensemble; trio.*

pianoforte (It.) see *piano.*

piatti (It.) see *cymbal.*

Picardy third the raised mediant at the end of a composition written in a minor key. The result is that the composition ends on a major chord. See also *chord; triad.* See illustration, page 168.

piccolo a wind instrument smaller than the flute and pitched one octave higher. It is used in orchestral scores and in military bands. Constructed of metal, the piccolo is the highest pitched of all instruments in the orchestra. See also *flute; wind family.* See illustration, page 168.

piccolo flautín (Sp.) see *piccolo.*

Picardy third

piccolo

piccolo flöte   (G.) see *piccolo.*

pick   see *plectrum.*

pieno   (It.) full.

piffeto   (It.) see *fife.*

pipe   **(1)** a cylinder that, as part of the organ, creates various pitches by vibrations of air. **(2)** a wind instrument's body, or a simple wind instrument with no keys or valves. See also *organ; wind family.*

piston   **(1)** a device on the organ used to activate preset registers on one or more manuals. **(2)** on brass instruments, the valves, which are operated to achieve varying pitches. See also *brass family; organ; registration; valve.*

pitch   **(1)** the high or low degree of a note or a series of notes. Pitch is described in terms of frequency, degree, alphabetical title, or fasola name. **(2)** descriptive of the quality and accuracy of a tone, with concert pitch the standard for tuning of other instruments. **(3)** an explanation of the ability of certain musicians to identify the exact value of a sounded tone (absolute, or perfect pitch); or to estimate tone names in relation to other sounded pitches (relative pitch). See also *absolute pitch; acoustics; fasola; note; perfect pitch; relative pitch; tone.*

pitch names   the alphabetical or fasola names assigned to each tone of the scale. See also *fasola; note; scale; solmization; tone.*

pito   (Sp.) see *whistle.*

pivot chord   a chord that exists in more than one key. When modulating, the pivot chord is the last chord belonging to the previous key, and the first introduced chord in the new key. It is also called the hinge chord or the common chord (not to be confused with the "common" triad in position one, three and five).
   An example of the pivot chord's use: When modulating from C major to B-flat major, F major is a pivot chord. It represents the subdominant chord in the key of C and the dominant chord in the key of B-flat. See also *chord; modulation.*

---

pivot chord

---

pizzicato (pizz.)   (It.) instruction to pluck the strings (used for violin, viola, cello and double bass) rather than bowing. When a pizzacato section is ended, the instruction "arco" tells the performer to return to bowing. See also *arco; string family.*

Plagal mode   any Church mode that begins on the fourth degree below the final (tonic), and extends upward to the fifth degree above. In comparison, an authentic mode is one that begins and ends on the tonic. See also *authentic mode; Church modes; mode.*

plainsong (alt. plainchant) a single-line melody (monophonic) that evolved into the Gregorian chant. The term is associated with western liturgical music, and is not applied to earlier musical forms of other cultures. See also *Ambrosian chant; Gregorian chant; liturgical music; monophonic sound.*

platillo (Sp.) see *cymbal.*

plectrum (1) a wooden, metal or plastic device used to pluck the strings of fretted instruments, such as the guitar. In popular use the plectrum is also called a pick. (2) part of the harpsichord's action, that plucks strings in response to the depression of a key. See also *action; fret; guitar; harpsichord; string family.*

polonaise (Fr.) "Polish," a dance in 3/4 meter of a noble or heroic character. The form, used in suites or as singular compositions, dates from the 17th century. See also *dance; suite.*

polychoral a choral work for two or more choruses. See also *choral; vocal music.*

polychord a chord that actually is the combination of chords in two different keys, found in atonal and bitonal compositions. For example, a chord involving the notes E-flat, F, G, A-flat, B-flat and C is the combination of an E-flat major chord (E-flat, G, and A-flat) and an F minor chord (F, A-flat, and C). See also *atonal music; bitonality; chord.*

---

polychord

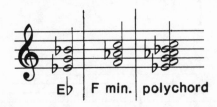

Eb | F min. | polychord

---

polymeter the use of different meters at the same time, to create special effects and offsetting rhythms, a popular device in 20th century music. For example, one part is written in 3/4 and another in 5/4 meter. In comparison, polyrhythm is the utilization of conflicting rhythms within a single meter. A polymetric effect can be created with different key signatures, or the use of irregular groupings. See also *irregular grouping; meter; rhythm.* See illustration, page 171.

polymodality descriptive of a composition employing two or more Church modes at the same time. In comparison, polytonality (or, bitonality) is the simultaneous use of separate modern keys. See also *bitonality; Church modes; mode.*

polymeter

dissimilar meter

irregular groupings

---

polyphony   music with two or more distinct lines of melody and harmony, each with its own rhythm, timing and characteristic sound. See also *counterpoint; harmony; homophonic sound; monophonic sound; rhythm; texture.* See illustration, page 172.

polyrhythm   the use of dissimilar rhythms, to create unusual accents or a sound similar to polymeter. However, polyrhythm occurs in a single meter. See also *cross rhythm; rhythm.* See illustration, page 172.

polytonality   the simultaneous use of several different keys. Bitonality (the use of two keys) is common in 20th century music, while true polytonality is relatively rare. See also *bitonality; key; tonality.*

pomposo   (It.) stately.

polyphony

polyrhythm

pop (popular) music with wide approval and appeal in the current day or, in one sense, any informal form of music using popular instrumentation, harmonies and rhythms. See also *folk music; jazz; rock 'n' roll.*

portamento (It.) a smooth glide from one note to the next, that can be achieved on only a few instruments, such as the violin, trombone, tympani, and vocally. The gliding quality is not the same as the glissando, which is a rapid sounding of progressive but distinct tones. See also *appoggiatura; glissando; vocal music.*

portato (It.) a method of performance approximately midway between legato and staccato. See also *legato; staccato.*

posaune (G.) see *trombone.*

position (1) the placement of notes in a progression, relative to one another; the design or appearance of a line of music. (2) the inversion of a chord or placement of notes in an octave, above or below the other notes in the chord. Positions of the chord include the root (tonic in the base), first (3rd in the base), 2nd (5th in the base) and 3rd (7th in the bass). (3) the placement of fingers of the left hand while playing stringed instruments. (4) the degree of extension of the trombone's slide, with the first position representing the least amount of extension. See also *chord; fingering; inversion; line; note; string family; trombone.*

position (inversion)

root　　1st　2nd　3rd

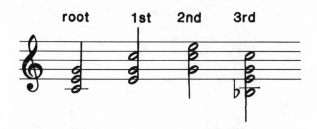

position (chord)

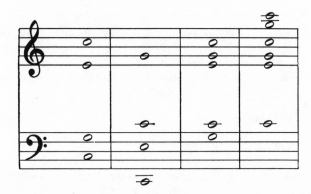

postlude a section played at the conclusion of a composition, or music to be performed on the organ at the end of a church service, while the congregation is leaving. See also *liturgical music; organ.*

prelude (1) name sometimes assigned to the overture of an opera; introduction to a fugue or suite; or an initial, short introductory movement of a symphony or other orchestral work. (2) music for organ, piano or ensemble played before a church hymn, also called a chorale prelude. (3) a character piece in one movement, usually for piano or other solo instrument. See also *character piece; fugue; introduction; opera; overture; suite; symphony.*

preparation a nonharmonic tone in which a harmonic note is suspended (held) from a consonant chord. It becomes dissonant as a subsequent chord is sounded, and finally resolves, either by changing, or through being held until a third chord is sounded. Preparation is an inverted form of suspension. See also *nonharmonic tone; resolution; suspension.*

---

preparation

---

prepared piano a piano whose strings have been altered in some way. Either pieces of metal, wood, felt, or other objects have been added to mute or alter sound quality; or actual tuning has been changed from the normal degrees. This is done to create a special effect in music performance or interpretation. See also *piano.*

prestissimo (It.) extremely fast.

presto (It.) very fast.

program music music that tells a story, without the accompaniment of vocal parts (spoken or sung). Music symbolically represents characters, emotions, ideas or events suggested by a storyline or title. Well-known examples of program music include the 1812 Overture (Tschaikowsky); Scheherazade (Rimsky-Korsakoff); and Night on Bald Mountain (Moussorgsky). See also *symphonic poem.*

progression the changes in chords and harmony, with a logical order and purpose. For example, when modulating from the key of G major to the key of C major, the progression of G, D7, G7, C is logical, and achieves the desired effect. See also *chord; harmony; modulation.* See illustration, page 175.

progression

---

progressive jazz   a jazz style popular during the 1950s and 1960s, employing a smooth sound quality. Previously, jazz sounds had been relatively harsh. The newer style is also referred to as "cool" jazz. See also *jazz.*

progressive tonality   the practice of beginning a composition or movement in one key, and ending it in another, often with several modulations in between. See also *key; modulation; tonality.*

prologue   the introduction to an opera, no longer in style. It often was included for the purpose of explaining the plot or to acknowledge and welcome patrons in attendance. See also *introduction; opera.*

psaltery   a medieval stringed instrument that had features of the dulcimer, lyre and zither. See also *string family.*

puzzle canon   a canon which included only the first voice in written form. Performers figured subsequent parts on their own. See also *canon.*

Q

quadruple counterpoint   type of counterpart where one or more of four distinct voices is transposed with other voices. For example, a lower part becomes an upper part, as the result of one part moving by an interval of one octave. See also *counterpoint; invertible counterpoint.*

quadruple fugue   a fugue with four separate themes, each of which is developed in fugue form. See also *fugue.*

quadruple meter　all meters with divisions of each measure into four beats, such as 4/2, 4/4, and 4/8 time. See also *meter.*

quadruplet　an irregular grouping of four notes, having the same time value as one full measure. The quadruplet appears in triple time, for example. While the normal beats are three per measure, one part is written in quadruplets. See also *irregular grouping; meter; polyrhythm; rhythm.*

---

quadruplet

---

quartal harmony　harmony constructed and based on intervals of the fourth, rather than on the third (tertian). See also *fourth; harmony; tertian.*

---

quartal harmony

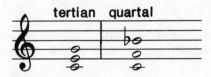

---

quarter note　a note representing time value equal to one-fourth the value of a whole note (in quadruple time), or one-third the value of a dotted half note (in triple time). See also *crotchet; note.* See illustration, page 177.

quarter rest　a pause in sound equal to one-fourth of a measure's full value in quadruple time or one-third of a measure in triple time. See also *meter; rest.* See illustration, page 177.

quarter tone　a tone halfway between two semitones. In a quarter-tone scale,

quarter note

quarter rest

each octave contains 24 notes. The voice, stringed instruments, and trombone are capable of producing quarter tone values. See also *semitone.*

quarter tone notation   the scale used for quarter tone music, consisting of 24 notes per octave. Variations of sharps and flats are used to indicate the quarter tone values. See also *note; semitone; tone.*

quarter tone notation

ascending

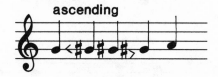

descending

quartet   **(1)** music written for four instruments or voices. **(2)** an ensemble of four performers. See also *ensemble; string quartet.*

quaver   see *eighth note.*

querpfeife (G.) see *fife*.

quintet a composition for five instruments or voices. See also *ensemble; string quintet*.

quintuple meter music containing five beats per measure. See also *meter*.

quintuple meter

quintuplet an irregular grouping of five notes, to be played within the time value of a measure or part measure with a count other than five. For example, in 3/4 time, the normal measure contains three beats. A quintuplet in 3/4 time involves five beats in the same time. See also *irregular grouping; meter; polyrhythm; rhythm*.

quintuplet

R

raganella (It.) see *rattle*.

ragtime music for the piano or other instrument, that became popular at the beginning of the 20th century and influenced developments in jazz music. It is characterized by syncopated rhythms in 2/4 or 4/4 time, and is as much a style of performance as a form of music. See also *jazz; piano; pop.*

rallentando   (It.) becoming slower.

range   the notes that can be sounded, from the highest to the lowest, on an instrument or by a singer.
   Instruments and voices are distinguished from one another in terms of their range, and by the strength and quality in sections of ranges. For example, many instruments tend to be weak and heavy in their extreme lower ranges, and strained in the extreme upper. An ideal middle range is strong, controlled and produces the most desirable tone color. See also *tone color; voice.*

rattle   a percussion instrument with a revolving cog and a wooden or metal spring. It is used in orchestral scores for sound effect. See also *percussion family.*

ray   the name of the second degree in the diatonic scale, in the solmization system. See also *degree; solmization; supertonic.*

real answer   the response to a fugue's subject that exactly duplicates that subject, in the same key. In comparison, a tonal answer is one that occurs at an interval removed from the original subject (usually of a fifth or a fourth). See also *answer; fugue; subject; tonal answer.*

real answer

recapitulation   a repeat of the theme and exposition in sonata-allegro form music. The usual form involves the exposition (in the tonic key), followed by the development, and then the recapitulation (in the dominant key). See also *development; exposition; sonata-allegro form; theme.*

recitative   a style of singing arias and other vocal solos, in which the accompaniment is of secondary importance. Simple chords or limited harmonies may be used. Singers of recitatives may take liberties in the time and rhythm, to increase the dramatic impact of the words and mood. For example, the singer may substitute notes in place of those written, or add non-harmonic tones. The recitative is a dramatic singing style, interpretative in the same way that an actor may take liberties with the intended phrasing, motivation or wording in a play. See also *aria; opera; solo; vocal music.*

recognition of keys   the ability to name a key upon seeing the key signature, resulting either from memorization or by applying these rules:
   a. If a key signature contains sharps, the last sharp of the key signature is the leading tone of the key. Thus, the tone one half step above the last sharp is the major key's tonic. The minor key's tonic will always be one whole tone lower than the last sharp.

last sharp	major key	minor key
-	C	A
F	G	E
C	D	B
G	A	F♯
D	E	C♯
A	B	G♯
E	F♯	D♯
B	C♯	A♯

   b. If the key signature contains flats, the second to last flat is the major key's tonic note. The key of C (no flats) and F (one flat) must be memorized. However, most musicians quickly identify these keys from frequent use. The tonic of a minor key is exactly two whole tones higher than the last flat in the key signature.

last 2 flats	major key	minor key
—	C	A
-B	F	D
BE	B♭	G
EA	E♭	C
AD	A♭	F
DG	D♭	B♭
GC	G♭	E♭
CF	C♭	A♭

See also *flat; key signature; sharp.*

recorder   an instrument in the wind family, popular from the 16th to 18th centuries and, in limited applications, again in modern music. It is constructed of wood or plastic, and has a series of air holes. Four sizes and ranges are the soprano (descant), alto (treble), tenor, and bass. See also *fipple; flute; wind family.*

reduction   a piano score of the full ochestral parts, the purpose of which is to enable one performer to play a keyboard version. Playing from a full score is difficult, as the performer must view many parts and transpose from a variety of keys in which the parts are written. In the composition of orchestral music, the first version often is developed as a reduced score; parts are then orchestrated by the composed upon completion of the work. See also *condensed score; orchestral score; score.*

reed (1) a thin strip of cane, metal or other material, used to create a vibration in the air column of a wind instrument. The reed is employed in one of three ways:

a. free—allowed to vibrate without direct mouth contact or control, as in the harmonica.

b. single—as used in the clarinet and related instruments, or the saxophone.

c. double—as used in the oboe family.

(2) a classification of organ stops, or the register representing or approximating the reed and woodwind instruments. See also *organ; stop; wind family.*

reed instrument a family of instruments employing a reed to create and control vibration of the air column. Included in this group are the entire wind family (except the flute and piccolo). See also *wind family.*

refrain (1) a section of vocal music that recurs following each stanza. For example a song has three different stanzas. After each one has been sung, the refrain follows, in identical form each time. (2) a section in an instrumental composition that is repeated several times, as a bridge between movements; to signal the end of a section; or as a theme in rondo form. See also *chorus; folk music; pop; rondo form; vocal music.*

register (1) the combination of pipes on an organ that is activated by a single stop. (2) descriptive of the quality of sound in a range of an instrument or voice. See also *chord range; head voice; melody range; organ; range; stop; vocal music.*

registration the various combinations of sound that are possible with the use of organ stops. See also *organ.*

---

rehearsal mark

---

rehearsal marks symbols—letters, numbers, asterisks, and other marks—placed above the staff, to assist performers in locating a specific point in the score. Several systems are used:

a. Marking each point where a section begins or ends, or when other changes occur (such as the entrance of the brass section). This system enables performers to quickly locate likely points where the ensemble will begin during rehearsals.

b. Marks placed at every eighth measure, to correspond to the normal length of a musical phrase.

c. Marks placed at regular intervals, such as every 10th measure.

See also *measure; phrase.*

relative key   a key that shares several common chords and notes with another key. The closest key relationships exist between keys that (a) have the same key signature; or (b) are separated by a single sharp or flat in the key signature.

For example, the key of C major is closely related to:

-*A minor,* the relative minor (same key signature)

-*G major,* key of the dominant (one sharp, so that the two keys have six common notes out of seven)

-*E minor,* relative minor of the dominant (the same key signature as G major)

-*F major,* key of the subdominant (one flat, so that the two keys have six common notes out of seven)

-*D minor,* relative minor of the subdominant (the same key signature as F major)

-*C minor,* the parallel key (different key signature, but the same tonic note)

Modulating to a closely related key is simplified due to the similarities of the two subject keys. Tonal attributes of more distant keys require more elaborate preparation for a smooth change. See also *circle of fifths; key relationship; modulation; opposite mode; parallel key.* See illustration, page 183.

relative pitch   the ability to identify a pitch by its interval relationship to another pitch. For example, an individual with relative pitch, upon hearing the note C, will be able to identify a G by recognition of the interval of a perfect fifth. The ability also extends to chords. For example, after hearing a C major chord, the individual will correctly identify an F major, by recognition of the subdominant of the first chord. See also *absolute pitch; chord; interval; perfect pitch.*

Renaissance music   music written during the period from approximately 1450 through 1600, following the Gothic, or medieval and before the Baroque period.

Renaissance music was primarily vocal. The madrigal was a prominent form during the period, and advances in polyphonic forms were significant. See also *Baroque; Gothic period.*

repeat   (1) notation to exactly duplicate a section of music, including all notes, rests and other notation included in the section. When the repeat sign (two vertical dots, followed by a thin line and a thick line) appears, the performer is instructed to repeat from the point that the same sign appears in reverse (thick line, thin line, two vertical dots). If no reverse symbol is present, music is to be repeated from the beginning of the movement.

Repeats are written with additional notation and symbols. The repeat sign,

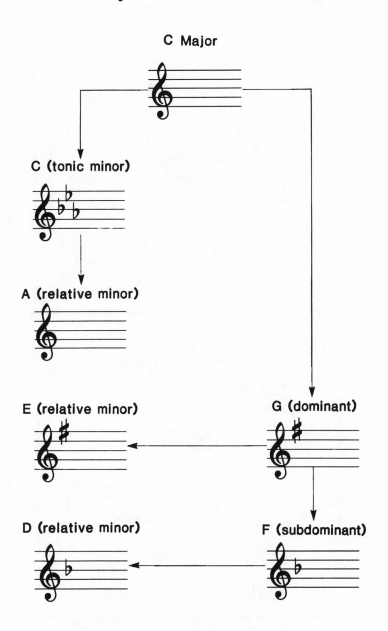

relative key

C Major

C (tonic minor)

A (relative minor)

E (relative minor)   G (dominant)

D (relative minor)   F (subdominant)

repeat (sections)

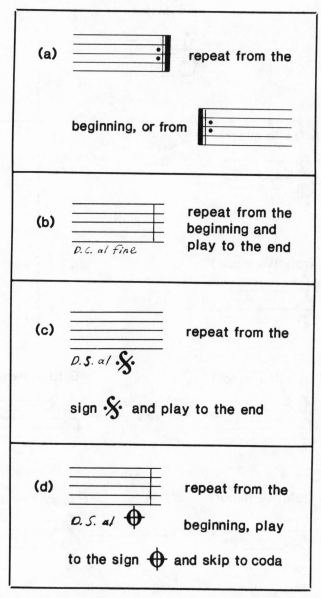

accompanied with the words, "D.C. al fine," means return to the beginning and play to the end. Other symbols are used to tell the performer to repeat from one point to another, and then to skip to the end.

repeat (notes and measures)

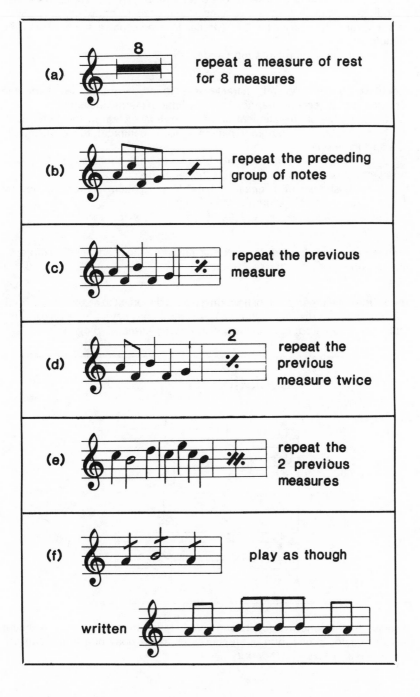

(a) repeat a measure of rest for 8 measures

(b) repeat the preceding group of notes

(c) repeat the previous measure

(d) repeat the previous measure twice

(e) repeat the 2 previous measures

(f) play as though

written

(2) notation instructing the performer to duplicate a measure, parts of a measure, rests, or a limited series of notes. Various symbols are used for this, including a number written above a measure containing an extended rest symbol; a vertical line offset by dots (similar to a percentage symbol); and the tremolo.

See also **Illustrated Notation Guide.**

repetition one of several characteristics found in music, involving the repeated use of sections, harmony, or rhythmic patterns, including:

a. the traditional restatement of the exposition section in sonata form.

b. duplication of a harmonic pattern in accompaniment, to establish unity or a specific mood.

c. recalling a recognizable series of notes to unify a thematic statement in a movement or composition, such as the leitmotiv.

d. establishment of a repeating bass rhythm pattern, as used in several dance forms; a notable example is the bolero.

See also *bolero; harmony; leitmotif; rhythm; sonata form.*

requiem music to be performed during a mass for the dead. See also *dirge; lament; liturgical music; mass.*

resolution the progression of harmony, from a dissonant to a consonant chord. For example, the dissonant dominant seventh chord naturally resolves to the tonic. See also *chord; consonance; dissonance; harmony; progression.*

---

resolution

---

resonance the sonority, quality and reverberation of sound. Each instrument has a resonator in one form or another, such as the body of a stringed instrument. See also *acoustics; sonority.*

rest notation instructing the performer to sound no notes for the indicated time. Each rest has a time value corresponding to the equivalent value of notes or full measures. See also **Illustrated Notation Guide.**

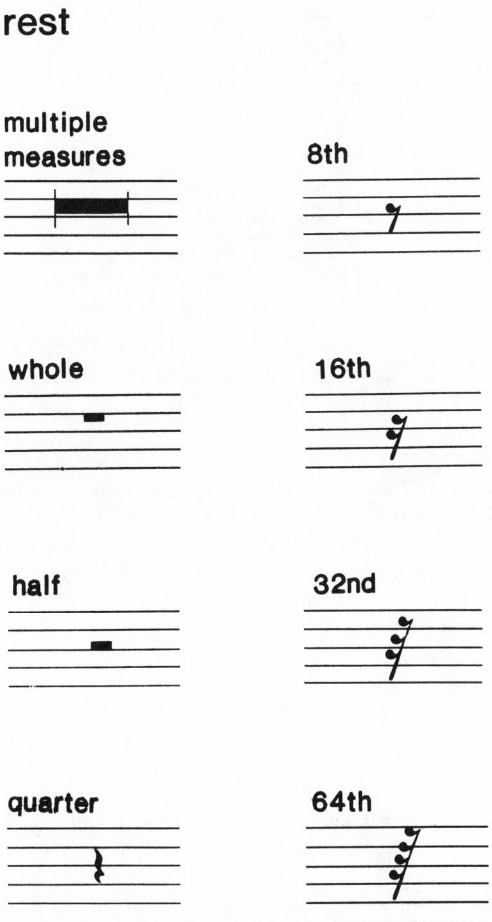

rest

multiple measures

8th

whole

16th

half

32nd

quarter

64th

resultant tone a third tone heard in some instances when two other tones are sounded loudly and at the same time. The frequency of the resultant tone is the difference between the frequencies of the other two tones. For example, when middle C (frequency 300) and the A above (frequency 500) are sounded, a resultant tone—if audible—will be the F below middle C (frequency 200). See also *acoustics; combination tones; differential tone; tone.* See illustration, page 188.

retenant (Fr.) holding back.

rhapsody a one-movement instrumental composition in fantasy, or free form,

resultant
tone

---

often suggestive of an improvisation. The rhapsody also may be of a nationalistic character or flavor. See also *fantasy; improvisation; nationalism.*

rhythm   the value, duration, and relationship of notes and other sounds (percussive) to (a) one another and (b) the timing of beats in each measure.

Rhythm is related to the motion of a line of music. For example, a melody in 4/4 time that employs only full-value quarter notes has a rhythm of four beats per measure, without variation. If this is continued for too long a time, the music becomes repetitive and uninteresting.

Variations in rhythm result from:

a. accented values.

b. irregular groupings.

c. combining dissimilar time signatures at the same time.

d. syncopation, the use of rests and dotted values, placing emphasis on the off-beat.

e. the combination of different values in two or more parts.

The rhythm of music is always relative. It becomes noticeable only when changed from one moment to another, or when two parts have offsetting rhythmic characteristics.

For example, a melody line proceeds in 3/4 time, with the accent on the first beat. It then changes to a rhythm in which the first beat begins with an eighth-note rest, and syncopated quarter notes follow, accenting the second beat. In another example, the melody notes fall on the measured beats, while harmony sounds on the half-beat. Rhythm is contrast in the timing and emphasis of beats, giving variety and flavor to music. See also *accent; beat; meter; motion; syncopation; time.* See illustration, page 189.

rhythmic mode   modes developed in the 13th century as a system for identifying possible rhythmic combinations. Six forms, all in triple time, were distinguished. In motets of the period, a rhythmic mode was introduced in one

rhythm

(a) accents

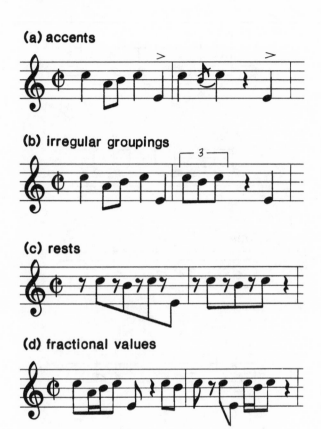

(b) irregular groupings

(c) rests

(d) fractional values

---

voice and carried through to the end. Other parts sang in the same, or in different modes at the same time. See also *mode; motet; triple time*. See illustration, page 190.

rinforzando (rfz.) (It.) stress on one note.

risoluto (It.) boldly.

ritardando (rit.) (It.) gradually reducing tempo.

rock 'n' roll music of jazz and folk origin, that became popular during the 1950s in the United States. Most rock 'n' roll originally was written for voice and guitar, often with drums added to provide a strong rhythm. However, expanded

rhythmic mode

first

second

third

fourth

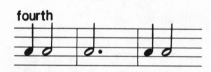

fifth

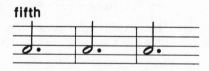

sixth

forms of rock 'n' roll today involve two, three or more guitars, electronic keyboard, and in some instances, orchestral instruments and multiple vocal parts. The structure of music has changed as well, from two- to four-chord repetitive progressions to elaborate and more complex forms. See also *folk music; jazz; pop; vocal music.*

rococo a transitional phase that occurred near the end of the Baroque period, and preceding the classical. It was characterized by superficial, decorative style and a tendency away from the serious musical forms of the Baroque period. See also *Baroque; classical.*

roll an effect produced on a drum by quickly altering strikes on the membrane with the drumsticks. See also *percussion family.*

romance a song, either vocal or strictly instrumental, of a sentimental character. See also *lullaby; song; vocal music.*

Romantic music the music of the 19th century, a period following classical and preceding the Modern period. Music stressed expression of emotions, often at the expense of the quality of music and its form. Developments in tonality eventually led to the atonal and bitonal trends of the 20th century. See also *classical; Modern period.*

rondo form music containing a primary section or theme (the episode, also called refrain), and one or more secondary sections or themes. In the most basic rondo form, the primary theme appears first and last, with one secondary section in between (the form ABA). However, in reference to classical sonata form, two or more secondary themes are more common, in various forms, such as ABACA or ABACABA. See also *episode; form; refrain; sonata form.*

rondo-sonata music combining features of both rondo and sonata forms. In place of the introduction of a third section or theme (as occurs in rondo form), the first section of rondo form (ABA) is followed by a development section (as in sonata form). Thus, the initial "ABA" is developed, and a second rondo form follows the development. The form may vary. For example, it may take either of the following sequences: ABA-dev-ABA, or ABA-dev-ACABA. See also *development; episode; form; refrain; sonata form.*

root the tonic, the note on which a scale is formed. For example, in the key of C major, the note C is the root. See also *scale; tonic.*

root

root bass   descriptive of harmony based entirely on chords in root position (tonic in the bass). For example, in the progression of chords C, G, F, and C, the tonic for each chord will appear in the lowest voice. See also *chord; position; tonic.*

---

root bass

---

root position   the position of a chord when the tonic appears in the lowest part, and the chord is comprised of intervals of the third. See also *chord; fundamental; inversion; position; triad.*

---

root position

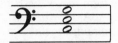

---

round   a simplified form of perpetual canon, with three or more voices sounding the same theme, in the same key, at staggered intervals. Upon reaching the end, each part may return to the beginning and start the round over. See also *canon; catch; perpetual canon.* See illustration, page 193.

rubato   (It.) freedom of style or tempo.

ruhig   (G.) quietly.

rute   (G.) see *whip.*

round

S

salon music   **(1)** simply composed and played character music, intended more for practice than as serious works. **(2)** difficult works, composed for accomplished singers or instrumentalists, but intended for private enjoyment rather than for public performance. See also *character piece; exercise; gebrauchsmusik.*

sassofono   (It). see *saxophone.*

saxofón   (Sp.) see *saxophone.*

saxophon   (G.) see *saxophone.*

saxophone   an instrument patented by Adolphe Sax in 1846, constructed of brass. Because of its use of a single reed (similar to that used for the clarinet), the saxophone is classified in the wind family. Rarely seen in orchestral scores, the saxophone is commonly used in bands and pop or jazz ensembles. The most widely used varieties include the soprano, alto, tenor, baritone and bass (others include the soprarino and C tenor saxophone). See also *jazz; pop; reed; wind family.* See illustration, page 194.

saxophone

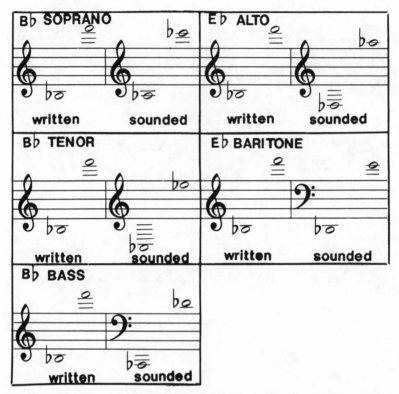

scale   a series of notes within a defined range, usually of one octave. The scale is identified in one of two ways: by its first note, or the tonic of the key in which the scale resides; or by its mode. In modern usage, mode is either major or minor; a scale may also apply to a Church mode. The mode determines the spacing of tones in the scale. The most common modes are:

a. major diatonic—eight tones, separated by whole tones at each degree except between degrees 3–4 and 7–8, which are separated by half tones.

b. minor diatonic—the major diatonic, but with a flattened third degree and, depending on the type of minor mode, other diminished degrees. Minor modes may be harmonic, melodic, or natural.

c. chromatic—12 tones, each separated by one half tone in an octave.

d. Church modes—characterized by whole and half steps at varying degrees, equated to tonic notes on each of the white keys of the piano.

e. pentatonic—a scale with five degrees in an octave.

f. whole-tone—a scale consisting six degrees in the octave, each separated by a whole tone.

See also *chromatic scale; Church modes; degree; hexachord; major scale; minor scale; mode; note; pentatonic scale; step; whole-tone scale;* and **Scales, Keys and Chords.**

scale degree the degrees of the scale, named for their relationship to the tonic or dominant. The purpose is to allow for comparisons of intervals to one another, regardless of the key in effect. See also *degree; dominant; harmonic analysis; interval; leading tone; mediant; subdominant; submediant; supertonic; tonic.*

scale degree

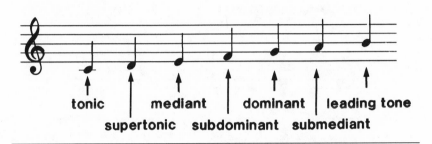

scena   a solo part of an opera, normally consisting of a recitative with an aria. See also *aria; opera; recitative; vocal music.*

schellen (G.) see *sleigh bells.*

schellentrommel (G.) see *tambourine.*

scherzando (It.) playfully.

scherzo (It.) a fast, lively minuet in a sonata or symphony. In some instances, one-movement compositions have also been given the name scherzo. In 3/4 time, it has the form of AABA. See also *minuet; movement.*

schiebe flöte (G.) see *slide whistle.*

schnell (G.) quickly.

schwindend (G.) dying away.

scie musicale (Fr.) see *musical saw.*

scordatura (It.) an adjustment in tuning of a stringed instrument to achieve a special effect, expand the normal range, or alter the tonality of tonal quality during performance. See also *string family; tuning.*

score **(1)** the notation of all instruments, written out for each part, or summarized in a condensed version. **(2)** as a verb, to write out the notes to be played by an instrument or sung by a voice; to orchestrate a work. See also *condensed score; notation; open score; orchestral score.*

second **(1)** the supertonic, the degree of the scale between the tonic (first) and mediant (third). **(2)** an interval of one whole tone (major second); one half tone (minor second); one and one-half tones (augmented second); or an enharmonic change only (diminished second). **(3)** descriptive of a part that is performed in support of a primary or melodic voice, or that assumes a secondary role in an ensemble (such as second violin). See also *degree; enharmonic; interval; supertonic.*

second (degree)

second (interval)

second inversion the position of a chord when the dominant (fifth) is in the lowest position. For example, a C major chord in the second inversion consists (from bottom to top) of G, C and E. See also *chord; inversion; position.*

second inversion

secondary dominant   the dominant of a key other than the subject key, indicated in harmonic analysis by Roman numerals. For example, when the key of C major is in effect, a D major chord is the secondary dominant of the key of G. This is indicated by the symbol "V of V" or "V/V." See also *dominant; harmonic analysis.*

secondary dominant

I   V V/V IV   I

section   **(1)** a group of phrases in music that, in the opinion of a performer, conductor, composer or observer, represents a distinct expression. **(2)** a group of instruments of similar construction, sound and method of sound production. In the orchestra, the major sections are strings, winds, brass and percussion. See also *orchestration; phrase.*

sectional   descriptive of musical forms in which phrases are easily identified by beginning and ending sections within a movement. In comparison, some musical construction involves phrasing that overlaps. See also *cadence; phrase.*

sega   (It.) see *musical saw.*

segno   (It.) a sign used to lead performers to a specified point in the score, from which a repeat section begins. See also *notation; repeat.*

segno

segue   (It.) proceed to the next section without pause.

semibreve   the English name for the whole note. See also *whole note*.

semibreve

semichorus   a secondary chorus, usually associated with vocal music. However, the term can be applied to instrumental groups as well. The semichorus is intended to offset or compliment a larger, primary group of singers or instruments. See also *chorus; vocal music*.

semiquaver   the English name for the sixteenth note. See also *sixteenth note*.

semiquaver

semitone   the difference in degree between two tones by a single chromatic degree; a half step. See also *degree; half step; interval; tone*.

semplice   (It.) simply.

septet   a composition for seven voices or instruments. See also *ensemble*.

septuplet   (alt. septimole) an irregular grouping consisting of seven notes, when the meter in effect is for a different number of beats. For example, a composition in 3/8 time will normally contain three eighth notes or the equivalent per measure. A septuplet calls for the sounding of seven eighth notes in a single measure. See also *irregular grouping*. See illustration, page 199.

sequence   the repetition of a figure or phrase in the same voice or part, at an interval above or below the original. If the sequence contains the exact intervals as in the original, it is a real sequence. However, if certain intervals are modified in respect of the key, it is a tonal sequence. See also *answer; phrase; repetition*. See illustration, page 199.

septuplet

sequence

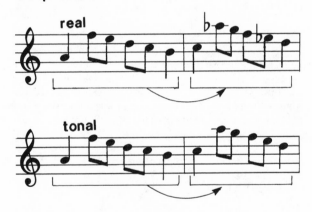

serenade **(1)** a ballad or love song. **(2)** a piece for limited instrumental ensemble, intended for performance outdoors. See also *ballad; ensemble; song.*

sereno (It.) serenely.

series in twelve-tone music, a form, also called tone row, in which all 12 chromatic notes are introduced in a specific order. The order is unchanging throughout the composition, although numerous variations are possible, such as sounding the series in inversion, retrograde, retrograde inversion, and transposition. When further modified in terms of rhythm, chord structure and polyphonic treatment, the variations are greater than in traditional tonal harmonies.

A series can refer to any grouping of tonal combinations, although its usage is normally applied to the 12-tone system developed by Arnold Schoenberg in the early 1920s. See also *form; tone row; twelve-tone music.*

series

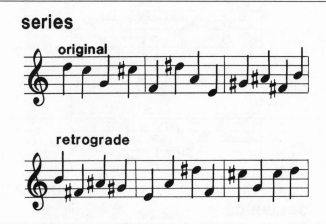

serrucho (Sp.) see *musical saw.*

seventh **(1)** the scale degree between the submediant (sixth) and tonic (octave); the leading tone. **(2)** an interval of seven steps, that may be major, minor, augmented or diminished. The minor seventh is reduced one half step from the major; the augmented is raised a half step; and the diminished is reduced two half steps, resulting in the enharmonic of a major sixth. See also *degree; enharmonic; interval; leading tone.*

seventh (interval)

sextet a composition for six voices or instruments. See also *ensemble.*

sextuplet (alt. sextolet) an irregular grouping of six notes, to be played in the same metric space as a grouping of a different count. For example, a composition is written in 4/4 time. A sextuplet calls for six notes, to be played in place of four. This irregular grouping is rare, since a triplet will usually suffice. See also *irregular grouping; triplet.* See illustration, page 201.

sextuplet

---

sforzando (sfz) (It.) (alt. sforzato) forced or reinforced; emphasis to be placed on one note or chord, with an immediate return to soft (piano) volume. See also *notation; volume.*

shanty (alt. chantey, chanty) a work song, with strong, regular rhythm. See also *chant; song.*

sharp notation to raise a pitch by one half step. See also *accidental; double sharp; flat; natural.*

---

sharp

---

shift moving from one position to another, on the frets of a stringed instrument, or by movement of the slide on the trombone. See also *position.*

side drum see *snare drum.*

sifflet (Fr.) see *whistle.*

sight read the performance of music on sight and without rehearsal. This ability, developed through practice, is valuable to performers of all instruments, and to singers. Highly capable sight readers are able to sight read as well as to transpose to different keys at the same time. See also *transposition; vocal music.*

signalhorn (G.) see *bugle.*

signature the identification shown at the beginning of a line of music, instructing the performer in (a) the key in effect (shown by the number of sharps and flats); and (b) the meter, or time signature, representing the number and type of notes per measure. See also *key signature; time signature.*

signature

similar motion a type of motion in which two parts move upward or downward together. However, the precise interval between the parts varies. In comparison, parallel motion involves movement in two parts in similar motion, when the interval remains unchanged. See also *consecutive interval; interval; motion; parallel motion.*

similar motion

simple interval an interval spanning one octave or less. See also *compound interval; interval.* See illustration, page 203.

simple meter all forms of meter involving simple duple time (2/2, 2/4); triple time (3/4, 3/8), and quadruple time (4/2, 4/4). See also *compound meter; meter.*

singspiel (G.) see *comic opera.*

siren a device used in the percussion section to create special effects in orchestral music; a shrill whistle that rises and falls in pitch. See also *percussion family.*

simple interval

sirena (It.) (Sp.) see *siren.*

sirena de pico (Sp.) see *slide whistle.*

sirena di fischietto (It.) see *slide whistle.*

sirene (G.) see *siren.*

sirène (Fr.) see *siren.*

sitar an Indian stringed instrument played with a plectrum. It contains from three to seven strings and has movable frets. The sitar is characterized by up to 12 sympathetic strings. See also *lute; plectrum; string family.*

six-four chord a chord constructed of a sixth and a fourth interval from the bass note. The second inversion of the triad is one example of this construction. For example, in the key of C major, the chord involves a G, C and E. The interval from G to C is a perfect fourth; and from G to E is a major sixth. See also *chord; inversion; second inversion.*

six-four chord

sixteenth note a note whose time value in 4/4 time is 1/16th that of a whole note (or one-fourth of a quarter note). A single 16th note contains two flags. Combinations have double beams. See also *note; time.* See illustration, page 204.

sixteenth rest a rest whose time value is the equivalent of a sixteenth note, indicated by a line with two flags. See also *rest; time.* See illustration, page 204.

sixteenth note

flag   beam

sixteenth rest

sixth **(1)** the submediant, or sixth degree of the diatonic scale. **(2)** an interval of six degrees, that can be major (a perfect fifth plus one whole step); minor (a perfect fifth plus one half step); augmented (a perfect fifth plus one and one-half steps); or diminished (the enharmonic equivalent of a perfect fifth). See also *degree; enharmonic; interval; submediant.*

sixth (degree)

sixth (interval)

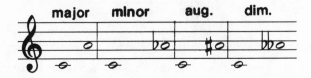

major   minor   aug.   dim.

sixty-fourth note   a note whose time value in 4/4 is 1/64th of a whole note (or 1/16th of a quarter note), often written as a grace note. Single 64th notes contain four flags, and combinations have four beams. See also *grace note; note; time.* See illustration, page 205.

sixty–fourth note

flag   beam

---

sixty-fourth rest   a rest whose time value equals a 64th note, indicated by a line with four flags. See also *rest; time.*

---

sixty–fourth rest

---

sleigh bells   a percussion instrument constructed of a strip of leather holding hollow metal spheres. Inside each sphere is a small metal ball. See also *percussion family.*

slentando   (It.) slowing.

slide   (1) a movable, U-shaped part of the trombone that enables the player to vary pitch, the equivalent of the valve on other brass instruments. Pitch is lowered by extending the slide outward and away from the performer:

position	description
first	open tone
second	one half step lower
third	one whole step lower
fourth	minor third lower
fifth	major third lower
sixth	perfect fourth lower
seventh	diminished fifth lower

   (2) a technique in performance of orchestral stringed instruments, in which the finger glides from one position to another.
   (3) a grace note in which two tones are sounded rather than one. It was used in 17th and 18th century music and was also called elevation. Notation consisted of (a) an "x" above the final note; (b) a trill-like mark between the initial and final

notes; (c) a line between the first grace note and the final note; or (d) the simultaneous writing of the first of two grace notes and the final note, separated by a slanted line.

See also *elevation; grace note; string family; trombone.*

---

slide (grace note)

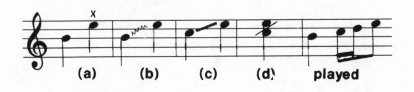

---

slide whistle   a percussion instrument whose tone can be sharply raised or lowered with a movable slide. See also *percussion family.*

---

slur

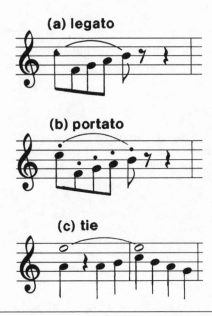

---

slur   a curved line extending from one note to another, used to indicate performance in one of three ways:

    a. legato, a smooth, continuous single phrase or statement without pause.

b. portato, performance of a series of staccato-like notes as a single phrase.

c. a tie, or the holding of a note over an extended time period, or between two or more measures.

See also *legato; portato; tie.* See illustration, page 206.

smorzando (It.) dying away.

snare drum a popular drum used in orchestral, band and popular music. It is constructed of a shallow, metal shell, connected from top to bottom with several metal strings (snares). These strings vibrate when the stretched membrane is struck. This drum is also called the military, field, parade, side, string, and trap drum. See also *drum; percussion family.*

soft pedal the far left pedal on the piano that, when depressed, reduces volume. This effect is achieved by shifting the action to the right, so that only one (or two) of the three strings are vibrated for each note being played. See also *piano.*

soh the fifth degree (dominant) of the diatonic scale, as named in the solmization system. See also *degree; dominant.*

solennel (Fr.) solemnly.

solmization a system of naming the degrees of the scale with single syllables in place of letters.

Two versions of solmization include the fixed and movable. In the fixed version, the syllables always correspond to the notes in the key of C major; in the movable, the syllables apply to degrees in all keys. See also *degree; fasola.*

---

solmization

doh   ray   mi   fah   soh   lah   ti   doh

---

solo (It.) alone, a featured instrument or voice. A section of music may include a solo passage with or without accompaniment. The term may apply to one individual performing within a larger ensemble; or to a sole performance, without other instruments or singers. See also *orchestration; vocal music.*

sonagli (It.) see *sleigh bells.*

sonata **(1)** a musical form developed during the Baroque period and still in popular use today. The sonata includes four distinct movements in one of two forms: Baroque and classical.

The Baroque sonata was written for small chamber ensembles. Movements one and three were slow; two and four were fast (church sonata form) or dances, much like the movements of the suite (chamber sonata).

The classical sonata included:

  a. first movement, in allegro tempo and sonata-allegro form.

  b. second movement, in slow tempo and sonata, binary or ternary form.

  c. third movement, a scherzo or minuet, in triple meter and ternary form.

  d. fourth movement, in allegro tempo and sonata-allegro or rondo form.

  (2) an 18th century composition for piano or other solo instrument. See also *Baroque; ensemble; form; movement.*

sonata-allegro form   a precise musical form used in the first movement (and other movements) of the symphony, concerto, sonata, and string quartet, also called sonata form.

In the most common version of sonata-allegro form, two themes are introduced in the exposition, and that entire section is repeated; this is followed by the development section; a final section, the recapitulation, repeats both original themes. In the recapitulation, themes appear in the dominant key, modulating to end the movement in the tonic.

In addition to these standard elements, the sonata-allegro form may include an introduction; episodes; and a coda. See also *concerto; development; exposition; form; recapitulation; string quartet; symphony.*

sonata form   alternate name for sonata-allegro form. However, this shorter title may be more accurate, since the form is used in movements of many tempos, and not just allegro movements. Use of the word allegro implies that the form is always to be played in fast tempo. See also *form; tempo.*

sonata-rondo form   see *rondo-sonata.*

sonatina   a short, simple sonata, usually for piano or other solo instrument. See also *piano; sonata.*

sonatine   (Fr.) see *sonatina.*

song   a short vocal composition with words as well as music. Songs for one singer and for larger groups have been prominent in operas, folk and popular music. See also *aria; folk music; opera; part song; pop; vocal music.*

song cycle   a composition of several movements, all vocal; a suite of songs. See also *suite; vocal music.*

song form   see *ternary form.*

sonority   the resonance of sound, as applied to:

  a. a range, such as the rich quality of an instrument or voice in a preferred or comfortable middle range.

b. strength in a given range, an instrument's capability for achieving power and volume.

c. a combination of tones in certain chords, which may have greater sonority in one inversion than in another.

See also *chord; range; resonance; voice.*

soprano **(1)** the highest voice that, in vocal music, is usually performed by female voice. However, in the 17th and 18th centuries, castrated males (castrato) maintained the soprano voice into maturity. Males can also achieve a soprano-like quality by singing falsetto; however, this effect lacks the power and quality desirable in vocal music.

Sub-groups of sopranos include coloratura and mezzo soprano. The quality and tone of the soprano voice led to further descriptive sub-groups, such as lyric or dramatic.

(2) the highest instrument in a group of similar instruments (soprano saxophone, for example).

See also *castrato; coloratura; falsetto; mezzo soprano; vocal music.*

---

soprano

average range

---

soprano clef an obsolete clef used during the 16th century for soprano voice, in which middle C was the lowest line of the clef. See also *clef; vocal music.*

---

soprano
clef

---

soprano saxophone one of several instruments in the saxophone family, that sounds one whole step lower than written. Although constructed of brass, the soprano is classified as a wind instrument, due to its use of a single reed. See also *reed; saxophone; wind family.* See illustration, page 210.

sostenuto (It.) sustained.

soprano saxophone

written   sounded

---

soundboard part of the piano and other keyboard instruments that resonates when strings are struck or plucked. See also *action; keyboard instrument; piano; resonance.*

soundpost small piece of wood connecting the top and bottom surfaces of stringed instruments. The purpose is to support the stretched strings, and to distribute vibration throughout the instrument's body. See also *resonance; string family.*

spacing the method of constructing a chord. Closely spaced chords in lower ranges, for example, produce a thick, indistinct combination of tones; wider spacing in bass parts is more desirable. See also *chord; inversion; position.*

spiccato (It.) separated, a technique in playing bowed string instruments. The bow is bounced off the strings rapidly as notes are sounded. See also *string family.*

spinato (It.) smoothly.

spinet **(1)** a small keyboard instrument with a single manual, similar to the harpsichord or virginal. **(2)** a modern style of upright piano. See also *harpsichord; keyboard instrument; piano; virginal.*

spiritoso (It.) spirited.

spiritual religious song of American folk origin. It may be in solo or multiple-part harmony. The spiritual is characterized by rapid tempo and syncopated rhythms. See also *folk music; vocal music.*

springer an "after-stroke," a form of grace note that appears following the subject note rather than before. It is the opposite of the appoggiatura. See also *appoggiatura; grace note; ornament.* See illustration, page 211.

staccato (It.) detached, a method of playing notes briefly and sharply. The

springer

effect is the equivalent of extremely short values, separated by rests. The staccato is notated with dots above the notes. See also *legato; notation.*

staccato

notated

sounded

staff five lines separated by four spaces, used for writing music in one of several clefs. The clef indicates the location of specific note values within the lines and spaces of the staff. Gregorian chants were written on four-line staffs, although the five-line version has been in use since the 13th century. Expanded staffs up to eight lines were used during the 16th century for keyboard compositions, to avoid excessive use of ledger lines. See also *bass clef; clef; ledger lines; note; treble clef.*

staff

stanza a complete verse of a song, sung from beginning to end. When more than one stanza is used, the identical music is used for each. See also *chorus; hymn; strophic form; vocal music.*

steel guitar a guitar whose sound is amplified electronically, used widely in pop and rock 'n' roll music. See also *guitar; electronic instrument; pop; rock 'n' roll; string family.*

stentando (It.) holding back.

step the separation of notes in an interval. Each of the chromatic degrees of the 12-tone octave are divided from one another by one half step. In describing an interval, the distance between the two degrees is said to contain a number of whole and half steps. Example: The C major third is separated by two whole steps. See also *chord; chromatic scale; half step; interval.*

sterbend (G.) dying away.

stop a device on the organ that activates and controls the registers. The stop on the modern organ is a switch or tablet. On older versions, stops were handles that were pulled out to activate registers. See also *organ; register.*

stopped tones produced on the horn by placement of the hand into the bell. This raises the tone a half step, and produces an exceptionally loud and unusual tone. Notation for stopped tones consists of a small cross, written above the note. See also *horn.*

stopped

stopping on stringed instruments, the depression of a string within a fret (guitar, lute, etc.) or at a position on the finger board (violin, viola, etc.). This reduces the length of the string, raising the pitch. See also *string family.*

stretto (It.) **(1)** the acceleration of themes in a fugue, so that answers overlap previous subjects. This technique is often used to increase intensity at the conclusion of the movement. **(2)** increasing the speed or doubling time values in a non-fugal composition, as a means for preparing for the ending; to vary intensity; or to develop a theme. See also *answer; development; fugue; subject.*

string bass see *double bass.*

string drum   alternate name for the snare drum; a drum with metal snares or strings, attached form top to bottom. The strings vibrate when the membrane is struck. See also *percussion family; snare drum.*

string family   a family of instruments on which sound is produced by bowing or plucking stretched wire or gut. In the orchestra, this family includes the violin, viola, cello and double bass. In pop and rock 'n' roll, guitars and other stringed instruments are used in many variations. Chamber ensembles may include the lute, mandolin, guitar and other instruments in addition to the more common orchestral strings.
   Keyboard instruments may be classified as belonging to the string family, since sound is produced by the striking or plucking of strings. They may also be considered as part of the definite pitch percussion family, since a key is struck or depressed. See also *cello; double bass; guitar; keyboard instrument; lute; mandolin; viola; violin.*

string octet   chamber ensemble made up of eight stringed instruments, usually four violins, two violas and two cellos; also called a double quartet. See also *cello; double bass; quartet; viola; violin.*

string orchestra   an ensemble composed entirely of stringed instruments, usually arranged in sections similar to those of the full orchestra (first and second sections of violin, viola, cello and double bass). See also *chamber orchestra; ensemble.*

string quartet   the most widely used ensemble in chamber music, comprising two violins, a viola, and a cello. In form and structure of music, the string quartet is the equivalent of a sonata for four strings. Quartets have been popular since the middle of the 18th century. See also *cello; chamber music; ensemble; sonata; viola; violin.*

string quintet   chamber music written for five string parts. The majority of quintets calls for two violins, two violas and a cello. In some cases, though, the ensemble consists of two cellos rather than two violas. See also *cello; chamber music; ensemble; viola; violin.*

string trio   a composition for three string parts, usually a violin, viola and cello. See also *cello; chamber music; ensemble; viola; violin.*

stringendo   (It.) increasing speed.

strophic form   a form in vocal music, in which each stanza is repeated with the identical music—melody, harmony, tempo and key do not vary. This form is popular in folk music and hymns. See also *art song; folk music; hymn; song; stanza; vocal music.*

style   **(1)** a recognizable method of composition, in which particular idioms, rhythms, harmony, instrumentation and form are identified with one composer or school of theory. **(2)** identification with a period of musical practice and theory. **(3)** the method of performing or interpreting a composition or of playing an instrument. See also *composition; form; idiom; interpretation; musical period.*

subdominant   the fourth degree of the diatonic scale, located a perfect fourth above the tonic. The name is derived from the interval created when the fourth degree is inverted with the tonic. In that inversion, it is a fifth (dominant) below (sub) the tonic. The fourth degree may be perfect, augmented or diminished. See also *interval; perfect interval; tonic.*

subdominant

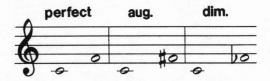

subito   (It.) suddenly.

subject   **(1)** a melody, theme or series of closely related notes that recur throughout a composition. **(2)** one of the two themes introduced in the exposition section of movements written in sonata form. **(3)** the antecedent of a fugue, in other voices. See also *answer; antecedent; fugue; melody; sonata form; theme.*

submediant   the sixth degree of the diatonic scale, also called the superdominant. The submediant, when inverted, is related to the tonic in the second degree, or the mediant. This degree may be major, minor, augmented or diminished. See also *degree; interval; tonic.*

submediant

subtonic   an alternate name for the leading tone, the seventh degree of the diatonic scale. See also *leading tone.*

suite a form of instrumental music originating during the Baroque period. It contains several short movements, often described as dances. In the modern suite, as composed since the mid–19th century, there tends to be a lesser degree of formality and restriction in form than in the earlier type. Many modern suites are composed as symphonic poems, or are derived from dances for the ballet. See also *Baroque; dance; symphonic poem.*

superdominant an alternate name for the submediant, the sixth degree of the diatonic scale. See also *submediant.*

supertonic the second degree of the diatonic scale. This degree may be major, minor, augmented or diminished. When diminished, the interval is the enharmonic equivalent of the tonic. For example, in the key of C major, a diminished second involves the notes C and D double flat. See also *degree; interval; tonic.*

supertonic

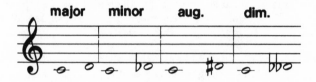

suspension a nonharmonic tone created when one note from a previous chord is held, while a new chord is sounded. This creates a dissonance, requiring resolution. See also *anticipation; nonharmonic tone.*

suspension

sustain pedal a third pedal on the piano (not always present), also called sostenuto. It is a variation of the damper pedal, enabling the performer to sustain a note or chord while playing subsequent, non-sustained notes. Example: The sustain pedal is depressed while a low C is played. Immediately after, a series of chords are played with both hands. As long as the sustain pedal remains depressed, the low C string will continue to vibrate. See also *damper; pedal; piano; sostenuto.*

swell (1) a manual on the organ. When only two manuals are present, swell is the top manual. When four manuals are present, the solo is on the top, so that swell becomes the second manual. (2) a device on the harpsichord or organ that controls volume, consisting of a series of shutters controlling sections of pipe. Operation occurs through a foot pedal. (3) the effect of increasing and then decreasing volume. See also *harpsichord; manual keyboard; organ; volume.*

swing a form of energetic dance or jazz ensemble performance, popularized during the 1930s. See also *band; dance; jazz; pop.*

syllables arbitrary names assigned to the degrees of the scale, for the purpose of identification. The fasola system employs one-syllable names for each degree of the scale, a method also called solmization.

Although several variations exist, the most common names (with spelling variations), ascending from the tonic, are doh, ray, mi, fah, soh, lah, and ti. Syllables are also assigned to sharps at each degree (example: di, ri fi, si, and li); and to flats (example: te, le, se me, and ra).

Syllables may be fixed or movable. In the fixed version, the note C is always the tonic doh (or, do). This rule applies regardless of the key in effect. Under the movable system, syllables refer to the degree of the scale rather than a specific note. Thus, "doh" is always the tonic. See also *fasola; notation; solmization.*

sympathetic vibration a natural tendency of a string to produce sound spontaneously, when its tone is sung or played independently. For example, a note is depressed on a piano without being sounded. The identical tone is then sounded on another instrument. The piano's string will begin to vibrate. The same effect can be achieved on any stringed instrument. See also *piano; string family.*

symphonic poem a suite or, more often, a composition in a single movement, based on a literary or other non-musical idea; a musical interpretation of a theme or story. Many nationalistic compositions are symphonic poems. See also *nationalism; program music; suite.*

symphony a composition for full orchestra, a major form since the 18th century. The classical symphony contains four movements and employs sonata form for the first and last movements. Symphonies of fewer movements have been composed, including one-movement versions. The symphonic form was developed over time from several smaller and less elaborate ensembles, including the overture, concerto, string quartet and other forms of chamber music. See also *concerto; orchestra; sonata.*

syncopation a meter in which emphasis is placed on weak beats of each measure. For example, in 4/4 time, emphasis occurs on the third beat; or, in 3/4 time, on the second beat.

The effect is achieved in several ways:
a. with a tie. The strong beat is held over to a weak beat.
b. with the use of rests in strong beats.

c. with the use of accents.
d. with the use of dotted note values.
See also *jazz; meter; rhythm.*

---

syncopation

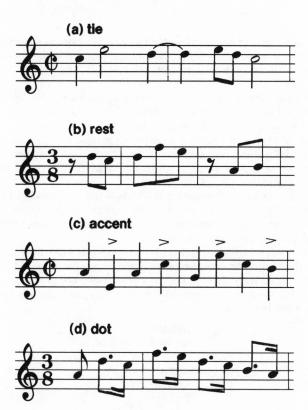

(a) tie

(b) rest

(c) accent

(d) dot

---

synthesizer an electronic device that enhances, alters, filters or otherwise controls musical sound and sound quality. These include:

a. signal modifiers—devices that filter sound or emphasize certain characteristics, reverberations, and decay mechanisms.

b. signal generators—devices that produce waveforms, such as the oscillator.

c. connecting devices created for voltage variation and control.

Modern use of synthesizers has advanced to the point that in some cases, the synthesizer is itself considered an instrument. See also *electronic instrument.*

system the combination of staffs used to show notation of multiple-part instruments, choir sections, multiple voices, and sections. The use of braces, brackets, single lines and double lines distinguishes the mix of voices and parts. See also *brace; great staff; staff;* and **Illustrated Notation Guide.**

T

tablature a method of notation in which letters, numbers or other symbols are used in place of notes. Varieties of the tablature system were in use from the 15th to 17th centuries and, in modern times, are still used in certain guitar and ukelele scores.

Tablature systems vary depending on the instruments. The obsolete forms of notation for lute were completely unrelated to one another, for example. In Italian and Spanish compositions (a), a six-line staff represented each of the lute's strings. An "o" was used to indicate open strings, while numbers, written on the appropriate line, showed which frets to depress. Rhythm was keyed above the staff by way of single notes or note multiples, and the highest line represented the lowest pitched string.

In French notation for the lute (b), the highest space represented the highest pitched string. Rhythm was shown by notes written above the staff, and letters were used for fret positions, written within spaces rather than on lines, as in the Italian and Spanish tablature system.

Guitar chords (c) are constructed on a grid, using dots for frets and fingering positions. The chord name is also abbreviated above the symbol block. Open strings are notated with a small, hollow circle above the grid, and strings not played lack dots or open string symbols. For example, an A minor seventh chord is notated, from bottom to top:

string	notation
E	no symbol (not played)
A	open string
D	second fret
G	open string
B	first fret
E	open string

See also *guitar chords; notation systems.* See illustration, page 219.

tacet (Lt.) silent, instruction that an instrument is not to be used during a movement or a long section of music. See also *notation; orchestration.*

tag the final ending. See also *coda.*

talon (Fr.) the lower section of a stringed instrument's bow, also called the frog or nut. See also *bow; frog; nut.*

tambor (Sp.) see *drum.*

tablature

(a) Italian and Spanish

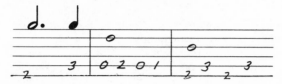

(b) French

(c) guitar chords

Am7

---

tambor vasco   (Sp.) see *tambourine.*

tambour   (Fr.) see *drum.*

tambour de basque   (Fr.) see *tambourine.*

tambourine   a drum with a hollow, rounded frame, to which loosely connected metal plates, or jingles, are attached. As the membrane is struck or the instrument is shaken, the jingles vibrate. See also *drum; percussion family.*

tamburo   (It.) see *drum.*

tamburo basco   (It.) see *tambourine.*

tampon   a drumstick with heads at both ends, held in the middle and used to create a roll on the bass drum. See also *drum; percussion family.*

tam-tam   alternate name for the gong, an indefinite-pitch percussion instrument. See also *gong; percussion family.*

temperament   the alteration of intervals from their natural pitch values, to expand the number of keys in which music can be performed. The system in use today divides the octave into 12 equal sections, whereas natural tones in each key are not of the identical pitches as those sounded. Example: The true pitch of G-sharp is not identical to the true pitch of A-flat. However, on most equally tempered instruments, these pitches are enharmonic equivalents. See also *enharmonic; equal temperament; interval; just intonation; mean tones; unequal temperament.*

temple block   see *Chinese block.*

tempo   (It.) time, the pace of a composition, indicated by words (allegro, adagio, andante) or, less frequently, by metronome marks, showing the exact number of beats per minute. See also *metronome mark.*

tempo marks   words or phrases used to instruct performers as to the appropriate speed of a composition or movement. These may be written in any language, although Italian is commonly used and widely accepted for tempo. Some of the more common tempo mark names are:

mark	*speed*
presto	very fast
allegro	fast
moderato	moderate
andante	rather slow
adagio	slow
largo	very slow

See also *notation.*

teneramente   (It.) tenderly.

tenor   the highest male singing voice, above baritone and bass. See also *voice.*

---

tenor

tenor clef a clef used for the tenor voice, to avoid excessive ledger lines or changes in clef signs. The symbol is the same as the alto or viola clef; however, it is placed on third space of the clef. This placement means that the third space represents middle C. In modern music, tenor parts are written in treble clef, and sung an octave below the written note. See also *clef; voice.*

tenor clef

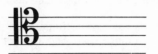

tenor drum an indefinite pitch percussion instrument larger than the snare drum but smaller than the bass drum. See also *drum; percussion family.*

tenor saxophone an instrument constructed of brass but classified in the wind family, due to its use of a reed similar to that of the clarinet. See also *reed; saxophone; wind family.*

tenor saxophone

tenor trombone the correct full name of the trombone used in the orchestra or band ("tenor" distinguishes this instrument from the bass trombone). See also *brass family; trombone.*

tenor trombone

tenuto (It.) hold; instruction to sound a note for its full value or, in many instances, for longer than full value. See also *notation*.

ternary form music written in three sections, with the third serving as a repetition of the first. Ternary may be described as having the form ABA or AABA (when the initial theme is repeated at the start). In comparison, binary form involves two themes, one followed by the other. See also *binary form; form*.

tertian harmony based on intervals of the major and minor third; the most familiar form of harmony in Western music. See also *harmony; interval; triad*.

tessitura (It.) the range of a voice or instrument that is most often employed, as compared to a maximum range span. See also *compass; range; voice*.

tetrachord (1) term describing a pattern of notes in Greek modes, consisting of two whole tone intervals and one half-tone interval, in descending order. (2) in modern usage, any segment of the scale involving four notes played in consecutive order, either ascending or descending. See also *chord; Greek modes*.

---

tetrachord

---

texture the combined melodic and harmonic structure of music. Melody (also referred to as "horizontal" texture) and chords or harmony (also referred to as "vertical" texture) determine the nature and structure of music, in one of three types:

    a. monophonic—an unaccompanied melody line.

    b. homophonic—melody accompanied by chords.

    c. polyphonic—two or more lines that consist of melody and secondary parts, each having their own independent rhythmic and melodic quality.

    See also *chord; homophonic sound; melody; monophonic sound; polyphony*. See illustration, page 223.

thematic index an index used to identify music not only by title and composer, but also by the opening measures of movements or compositions. This is a practical cross-referencing method, notably for works that are untitled or titled by numbers only (for example, Symphony Number 6 or String Quartet Number 11); or for distinguishing compositions by different composers, but with the same title.

    The thematic index may include notes actually written out in the key composed; or an alphabetical summary of notes in the melody, all represented in the key of C. See also *composition*.

texture

(a) monophonic

(b) homophonic

(c) polyphonic

theme   the melody or subject of a composition, that is introduced and then developed. See also *melody; subject.*

theme and variations   a musical form with multiple developmental treatment on a single theme. Variations may include modification to the melody, harmony, key, rhythm, contrapuntal accompaniment, ornamentation, mode, and combinations of changes. A theme may be performed in the style of a different composer or musical period. Variation may be thought of as a form of development; however, as an independent musical form, it allows greater freedom of departure from the original theme. See also *development; form; variation.*

theory   the rules governing structure and study of music. Theory encompasses the use of notation, keys and modes, key relationships, tempo, rhythm, texture, and tonality. It also establishes restrictions (such as the avoidance of consecutive perfect intervals in traditional theory, or the ban on breaking the established pattern of notes in the 12-tone system). See also *key; mode; notation; rhythm; texture; tonality.*

third   **(1)** the interval of three degrees from the tonic. A third may be major, minor, augmented or diminished. An augmented third is the enharmonic equivalent of a perfect fourth. And a diminished third, in which the upper note is reduced by two half steps, is the enharmonic equivalent of a major second. **(2)** the mediant, the third degree of the diatonic scale. See also *degree; enharmonic; interval; mediant.*

third (interval)

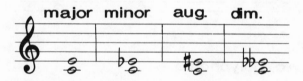

third (degree)

third inversion   a 7th chord in which the seventh appears in the bass position. See also *inversion; position; triad.* See illustration, page 225.

thirty-second note   a note whose value is equal to 1/32nd of a whole note. It is represented by a single note with three flags, or groupings of notes joined by three beams. See also *note; time.* See illustration, page 225.

third
inversion

---

thirty-second note

---

thirty-second rest   a rest with a time value equal to 1/32nd of a whole note, represented by a line with three flags. See also *rest; time.*

---

thirty-second
rest

---

thorough bass   a notation system for keyboard instruments in use during the Baroque period. Chords were represented by a series of numbers written beneath the bass clef. The performer improvised the right hand part, while completing the indicated chord in the bass. Abbreviations used in this system were numerous, including single numbers or numbers appearing one above the other. Some of the common symbols are:

symbol	chord
8	root position of the triad
6	first inversion of the triad
6 over 4	second inversion of the triad
7	root of the seventh
6 over 5	first inversion of the seventh
4 over 3	second inversion of the seventh
4 over 2	third inversion of the seventh

See also *basso continuo; continuo; figured bass; keyboard instrument.*

ti the seventh degree of the diatonic scale, in the solmization system, also called the leading tone. See also *degree; leading tone; solmization.*

tie a line connecting two notes, instructing the performer to hold the first note through the time value of the second. See also *notation; slur.*

---

tie

---

tierce de Picardie (Fr.) see *Picardy third.*

timbales (Fr.) (Sp.) see *tympani.*

time the beat of music, indicated by the time signature. See also *meter; rhythm; signature.*

time signature notation concerning the number and type of beats per measure. The signature contains two numbers, one above the other. The top number shows the number of beats, and the bottom one shows the type of note. Example: A time signature of 3/2 calls for three half notes per measure; a time signature of 2/8 calls for two eighth notes per measure. See also *meter; signature.*

timpani see *tympani.*

toccata (It.) a composition for the keyboard, originated during the Baroque period. The toccata often includes features designed to demonstrate the performer's abilities, or to show the full range and capability of the instrument. See also *instrumentation; keyboard instrument.*

tom-tom a primitive, single-headed drum, played by hand or with sticks. See also *drum; percussion family.*

tonal answer the response to a fugue's subject that duplicates notes at an interval removed from the subject's range, usually a perfect fourth or fifth. In

tonal answer

comparison, a real answer is a response in the same key, usually an octave below or above the subject. See also *answer; fugue; real answer; subject.*

tonal imagery   the ability to perceive, or to visualize sound and harmony by viewing a score; to hear music inwardly. See also *ear training.*

tonality   **(1)** the key, or tonal identification of music resulting from the relationship of chords and harmonies within the key. Example: The progression of chords C-G-F-G7-C establishes the tonal center in the key of C major. **(2)** the use of a single key in a composition, or of modulations from specific keys to other keys, to create singularity of tone. In comparison, atonal music avoids key identification. All keys and notes have equal importance, and no one tonal center is identified. See also *atonal music; bitonality; key; polytonality.*

tone   **(1)** the quality of a musical sound, involving judgment of pitch, tone color, duration, range, and intensity. **(2)** a whole tone, term used in England. **(3)** the sound that is heard. In this meaning, a tone is heard while a note is seen or read. **(4)** used interchangable with "note" in the United States. See also *note; pitch; whole tone.*

tone cluster

tone cluster   a chord or group of tones in close intervals, that creates a dissonance. This device is used in atonal music. See also *atonal music; chord; dissonance; interval.*

tone color   the relative strength and sound quality of a tone, when compared to the identical tone as performed by a different instrument or voice. Tone color is determined by pitch; volume; duration; the positioning within the range of the instrument or voice; and by the harmonics that the tone produces. See also *harmonic series; range; voice.*

tone painting   a composition that represents a musical interpretation of a theme, emotion or idea. See also *symphonic poem.*

tone row   the presentation of all 12 chromatic notes, used in 12-tone music, also called a series. The sequence of tones as first introduced does not change during the movement or composition, although multiple variations are possible, by way of changes in octave; rhythm; starting point; inversion; and retrograde inversion. See also *atonal music; series; twelve-tone music.*

tone row

tonguing   the articulation of notes during performance of wind instruments. See also *wind family.*

tonic   the first degree of the scale, whose name also identifies the key. From tonic to octave (a repeat of the tonic) is a perfect interval. See also *degree; final; key; perfect interval; scale.*

tonic

touch   the method employed in piano playing, by depressing keys to vary volume. See also *piano.*

tranquillo   (It.) calmly.

transcription the arrangement of a composition in a form other than as originally written: for different voices or instruments, in a more elaborate style, or in a different mode. See also *arrangement*.

transition (1) a section of music, also called a bridge, that connects two different movements. (2) the process of modulating from one key to another. See also *bridge; modulation*.

transposing instrument an instrument for which the written notes are not the same as the note values actually sounded. For example, the B-flat clarinet sounds one whole step lower than as written. The purpose is to avoid excessive ledger lines for instruments in ranges that fall between staff ranges. The transposition system originated because many instruments of the 18th century and before could be played only in their natural keys. See also *instrumentation; nontransposing instrument*.

transposition the duplication of musical pitches and harmonies, exactly in the intervals written but in a different key. The purpose may be to simplify performance (avoiding many accidentals), to adjust to the comfortable ranges of voices, or when an original instrument is replaced with another with a more restricted range. See also *accidental; range*.

---

transposition

original

transposed

---

traurig (G.) (alt: trauer) sadly.

treble clef the clef used for soprano and tenor voice, or for melody parts, also called the G clef. With this clef, the second line from the bottom is the note G natural. See also *bass clef; clef*. See illustration, page 230.

treble clef

G

---

tremolo   (It.) **(1)** notation for the rapid repetition or alternating of notes:

a. stringed instrument notation on a single note with diagonal lines through the stem indicates that the note is to be played with rapidly alternating up- and down-bows.

b. in keyboard notation, two joined notes with diagonal lines between the bars indicates rapid alternation between the two notes.

(2) often used inaccurately to describe a singer's vibrato.

See also *keyboard instrument; string family; vibrato;* and **Illustrated Notation Guide.**

---

tremolo

---

triad   a chord of three notes, built on the fundamental, or key note. A triad may be:

a. major, built on a major and a minor third. Example: In the key of C, a triad consists of C, E, and G.

b. minor, built on a minor and a major third. Example: In the key of C, a triad consists of C, E-flat, and G.

c. augmented, built on two major thirds. Example: In the key of C, an augmented triad consists of C, E, and G-sharp.

d. diminished, built on two minor thirds. Example: In the key of C, a diminished triad consists of C, E-flat, and G-flat.

See also *chord; common chord; fundamental; interval.*

triad

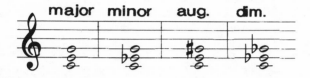

triangel   (G.) see *triangle.*

triangle   a three-sided, metal percussion instrument that is suspended on a hook and struck with a small hammer. Its pitch is indefinite, and it produces a high, clear sound. See also *percussion family.*

triangolo   (It.) see *triangle.*

triangulo   (Sp.) see *triangle.*

trill   an ornament instructing the performer to rapidly alternate the pitch of the subject note with the pitch of the note immediately above. This may create either a half tone or a whole tone, depending on the key and position of the subject note, and may be altered by special instructions from the composer. Notation is written with (a) a small waving line, or (b) the letters "tr." See also *percussion family.*

trill

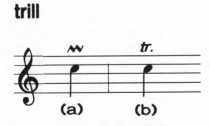

trio   (It.) **(1)** a composition for three voices or instruments, or in three movements. **(2)** an ensemble of three people. **(3)** in the minuet, the second of three sections, traditionally composed in three-part harmony. See also *ensemble; harmony; vocal music.*

trio sonata **(1)** a keyboard composition for one performer, containing three movements, themes, or sections. **(2)** chamber music in sonata form but written for an ensemble of three instruments. This form usually called for two melodic parts and one supporting, bass part. See also *chamber music; ensemble; keyboard instrument.*

triple counterpoint a form of invertible counterpoint that contains three parts. Inversion occurs when a high part is inverted into the bass. Example: In a contrapuntal trio, the first voice is introduced and is later lowered a full octave, so that it then provides the bass part to the other voices. See also *counterpoint; invertible counterpoint; texture.*

triple fugue a fugue in which three different themes are introduced and developed. This may occur simultaneously or, more often, in successive thematic order. Example: The first theme is introduced and developed, followed by the same pattern for themes two and three. The fugue concludes with a restatement of the first theme. In this case, the form of the fugue is ABCA. See also *couterpoint; fugue; polophony.*

triple time meter built on divisions of three beats per measure. Simple meter is any count with three beats; compound meter involves higher divisions of three beats (6, 9, or 12). See also *compound meter; meter; simple meter; time signature.*

---

triple time

simple

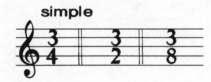

compound

---

triple-tongue a technique for articulation on wind and brass instruments. Notation usually appears only in instructional scores. In orchestral performance, the tonguing method depends on the speed and nature of the music. See also *brass family; tonguing; wind family.* See illustration, page 233.

triplet an irregular grouping of three notes, sounded in the same time that a different number of notes would demand. Example: In 4/4 time, the quarter

triple-tongue

notes of the first three beats are represented by triplets instead of quarter, eighth or sixteenth notes. See also *irreglar grouping; rhythm.*

triplet

tritone   an interval of three whole tones, equivalent to either (a) an augmented fourth or (b) a diminished fifth. See also *interval; whole-tone scale.*

tritone

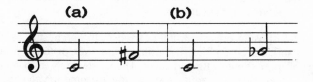

tromba   (It.) see *trumpet.*

trombón   (Sp.) see *trombone.*

trombone   a non-transposing brass instrument played with a slide in place of valves. As the slide is moved in toward the player, it reduces the tube's length and produces higher notes; as the slide is extended away from the player, the tube is lengthened and lower sounds are produced. At any slide position, the notes of the applicable harmonic series can be sounded. Two common varieties are the tenor and bass trombone. See also *bass trombone; brass family; harmonic series; non-transposing instrument; slide; tenor trombone.*

trombone

tenor

bass

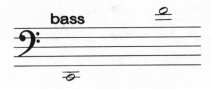

trommel (G.) see *drum.*

trompeta (Sp.) see *trumpet.*

trompete (G.) see *trumpet.*

trompette (Fr.) see *trumpet.*

troubadour minstrels and poet-musicians in southern France during the 12th to 14th centuries. Their songs were monophonic or, if harmonies were employed, they are not known today. Most troubadours wrote and performed their own music, and were members of the nobility. See also *minstrel; monophonic sound; song; vocal music.*

trumpet a transposing brass instrument used in the orchestra, as well as in dance bands and jazz ensembles. The trumpet has three piston or rotary valves and a range of approximately three octaves. The most widely used version is the B-flat trumpet. See also *brass family; transposing instrument; valve.* See illustration, page 235.

tuba a non-transposing brass instrument that plays the bass part. The orchestral tuba's range extends from the low F, upward for approximately three octaves. Several other varieties of tuba include the double-bass (lower range) and tenor, or euphonium (higher range). The tuba has either four or five valves. See also *brass family; non-transposing instrument; valve.* See illustration, page 235.

trumpet

tuba

tune (1) a melody or folk song. (2) correctness of pitch, describing an instrument as being in or out of tune; to tune, or adjust an instrument's pitch. See also *folk music; melody; pitch.*

tuning the adjustment of pitch, usually by tightening or loosening of string tension, or fit of a mouthpiece. See also *pitch.*

tuning fork a metal device that, when vibrated, produces a pure tone. For example, a tuning fork set to A-natural will vibrate 440 times per second. See also *absolute pitch; harmonic series; pitch; tone.*

turn a four-note ornament made up of the subject note, the note above, and the note below. Sequence is determined by the position of the subject note and the note to follow. See also *embellishment; grace note; ornament.*

turn

tutti (It.) all instruments; full orchestra.

twelve-tone music a modern technique of composition without a distinct key. Equal importance is given to all 12 tones of the chromatic scale. This technique was developed by Arnold Schoenberg during the 1920s. No note is repeated in a series (also called tone row) until all 12 tones have been sounded. Once a series is introduced, the sequence is not changed during the course of the movement or composition. The pattern can be altered, however, in a number of ways: by transposition, rhythmic, harmonic, and dynamic changes. Twelve-tone music allows for much greater variety than the more restrictive major and minor modes. See also *atonal music; series; tone row.*

two-part form see *binary form.*

tympani (alt. timpani) percussion instruments with definite pitch, which can be altered by varying the tension of the skin. This is accomplished with a key (on older versions) or a pedal on the modern drum (also called chromatic tympani).

    The skin is struck by a wooden stick with a head of felt or other material. In orchestral use, tympani consists of two drums, and often of three or more. They are frequently pitched in the tonic and dominant of the key in effect, although numerous changes in pitch may occur during performance. "Tympani" is the plural form of "tympano" (timpano).

    Spelling with a "y" is a common form, although the correct spelling is with an "i"—timpani.

    The range of tympani varies with the size of the drum bodies, and extends from middle C and downward approximately two octaves. See also *drum; kettledrum; percussion family.*

---

tympani

U

ukelele (alt. ukulele) a fretted, four-stringed instrument similar in shape to the guitar, but smaller. Notation involves a form of tablature similar to guitar chords. See also *guitar chords; string family; tablature.* See illustration, page 237.

ukelele

open strings

---

unaccompanied **(1)** vocal music without the addition of instrumental parts, also called a cappella. **(2)** instrumental or vocal works, played either as solos or as solo passages within ensemble works. See also *a cappella; solo.*

unequal temperament one of several methods of intonation used in the 16th and 17th centuries, in which pitch values were partially adjusted. A limited number of keys could be used on unequally tempered keyboard instruments. In keys farther removed from the primary key range, the interval relationships between notes became less accurate. In the 18th century, these various mean tone systems were replaced with the modern equal temperament system. See also *equal temperament; just intonation; mean tones; temperament.*

unequal voices vocal music that includes both male and female parts. See also *vocal music.*

unison **(1)** the simultaneous singing of the same melody or part by several vocalists. **(2)** the sounding of the same pitch or at intervals of an octave, by two or more different instruments. **(3)** the interval of no steps; the prime interval. See also *interval; octave; vocal music.*

unruhig (G.) restlessly.

up beat **(1)** the weak beat of a measure that precedes the first full measure in a movement or composition. **(2)** the movement of a conductor's hand or baton in an upward motion, indicating the weak beat. See also *beat; down beat.*

---

up beat

up-bow   in string music, a performance direction that the bow is to be moved across the string in a pushing motion, away from the performer. In comparison, a down-bow is a pulling motion, toward the performer. The up beat is indicated by a V-shaped mark above the note. See also *bow; down-bow; string family.*

upright piano   a rectangular piano with the soundboard and strings placed in a vertical position. In the larger, wing-shaped grand piano, the soundboard and strings lay horizontally in the box. See also *piano.*

ut   the original syllable used to designate the tonic, or doh in the fasola system. The origin of this syllable is an 11th century Gregorian chant entitled *Hymn to St. John the Baptist.* A monk named Guide of Arezzo noticed that the first tone of each stanza in the chant started one step above the previous stanza. He assigned fasola names according to the first Latin syllable for each of the six stanzas: ut, re, mi, fa, sol, and la. The leading tone was added to this system when the hexachord of six tones was replaced with the modern seven-tone scale. The tonic "ut" was replaced with the modern "doh." See also *degree; doh; fasola; syllable; tonic.*

V

valve   a device on a brass instrument that, when depressed, enables the performer to sound all the notes of the chromatic scale. Depression of the valve increases the tube's length, lowering the pitch. See also *brass family; harmonic series; piston.*

valve horn   a brass instrument with valves, as distinguished from the natural horn, natural trumpet, or bugle. See also *brass family.*

variation   a modified version of a previously stated theme, by way or ornamental changes, altered rhythms or harmony, or other forms of development. See also *chaconne; theme and variations.*

veloce   (It.) quickly.

ventilhorn   (G.) see *valve horn.*

verse   a stanza of a song or the section that is sounded before the refrain. See also *refrain; song; stanza; vocal music.*

verto   (It.) opening; instruction to play the first cadence. See also *cadence.*

vibrafono   (It.) see *vibraphone.*

vibráfono   (Sp.) see *vibraphone.*

vibraphon   (G.) see *vibraphone.*

vibraphone   a definite pitch keyboard instrument played with padded mallets. Vertical resonators under the keyboard open and close electronically to create a vibrating and prolonged sound effect. The tone may be further sustained with the use of a pedal. See also *keyboard instrument; marimba; percussion family; xylophone.*

vibraphone

vibrato   (It.) a subtle variation in pitch produced on a stringed instrument by gently shaking the left hand as a string is depressed; or produced by singers with fluctuations of vocal chords or the mouth. See also *tremolo; string family; vocal music.*

vif   (Fr.) lively.

vigoroso   (It.) vigorously.

villenella   (It.) an unaccompanied song, similar to the madrigal, with multiple verses. See also *a cappella; madrigal; song; vocal music.*

viol   stringed instruments in popular use from the 15th to 17th centuries, preceding common use of the violin, viola and cello. Viols had six strings rather than the four found on modern orchestral instruments, tuned in intervals of the fourth, and with a middle interval of a third. Modern stringed instruments are tuned in intervals of the fifth. The most widely used viols were the treble, tenor, and bass. See also *string family.* See illustration, page 240.

viol

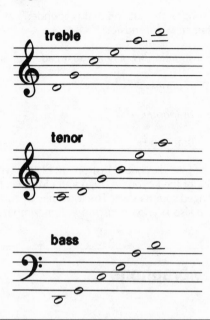

---

viol de braccio   (It.) viol "on the arm," a term for any stringed instrument held against the shoulder when played. See also *string family*.

viol de gamba   viol "on the legs," a term for any stringed instrument played while resting on the floor and played while in an upright position. See also *string family*.

viola   an instrument of the string family, of the same shape as the violin but slightly larger. It is tuned a fifth below the violin and has a range of approximately three octaves, starting with the C below middle C. Music for the viola is written on the alto clef, with the middle line representing middle C. Open strings are C, G, D, and A. See also *string family*.

---

viola

violin the most prominent instrument in the string family, tuned to open strings G, D, A and E. The violin has been in use since approximately 1600. Besides its broad range of nearly four octaves, the violin can produce a wide variety of effects and sound quality. The violin is played with a bow (or pizzicato). It is constructed of wood, and contains a body with a soundboard, back and ribs; the fingerboard and string holder; and the bridge. See also *bow; pizzicato; string family.*

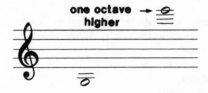

violín (Sp.) see *violin.*

violin family the ensemble used in string quartets and other chamber music for strings. Included are the violin (first and second parts), viola and cello. In orchestral music, the string section also includes the double bass. See also *ensemble; string family.*

violon (Fr.) see *violin.*

violoncelle (Fr.) see *cello.*

violoncello (It.) see *cello.*

violonchelo (Sp.) see *cello.*

violono (It.) see *violin.*

virginal **(1)** a 16th century keyboard instrument of the harpsichord family or, in a broader use, any keyboard instrument of the period. **(2)** a keyboard instrument similar to the harpsichord, but of various sizes and shapes, often called a spinet (although the preferred and more accurate use of "spinet" is in describing the wing-shaped member of the harpsichord family). See also *harpsichord; keyboard instrument; spinet.*

vite (Fr.) quickly.

vivace (It.) (alt. vivo) lively.

vivacissimo (It.) very lively.

vocal music   music composed for the human voice, including solos or songs for a combination of voices; numbers in operas, operettas, or musical comedies; or vocal sections in instrumental compositions. See also *aria; chorus; musical comedy; solo; song; opera.*

voce   (It.) voice.

voice   **(1)** the human singing voice, which produces sound by exhalation of air with vibration of the vocal cords, with resonance varied by changing the shape of the mouth. Note variation is produced by altering the tension of the vocal cords. **(2)** a line of music or part in an ensemble, with each instrument representing an independent voice. See also *ensemble; line; part; song.*

voice leading   the transition of vocal music from one chord to another, often through polyphonic variation in each part. See also *chorus; ensemble; line.*

voices   the distinct singing parts for female and male singers, including soprano, mezzo soprano, alto, tenor, baritone, and bass. See also *alto; baritone; bass; mezzo soprano; soprano; tenor.*

voicing   **(1)** an adjustment to a keyboard instrument's hammers to modify tone quality. **(2)** the arrangement of a chord or of different lines of music. See also *chord; keyboard instrument; line; tone.*

voile   (Fr.) subdued.

voix   (Fr.) voice.

volte   (It.) turn the page.

volume   the level of sound, indicated by abbreviated letters from ppp (pianississimo, or extremely soft) to fff (fortississimo, or extremely loud). See also *fortississimo; pianississimo.*

vuota   (It.) open string.

W

wachsend   (G.) increasing in volume.

waltz   a dance in triple time, usually of moderate tempo. Characteristics include a single bass note on the first beat, harmony on the second and third beats. One chord is harmonized per measure. See also *dance; tempo; triple time.*

wedge   a line of music in which the gaps between intervals increase progressively; contrary motion. See also *contrary motion; interval; motion.* See illustration, page 243.

wedge

---

well-tempered see *equal temperament.*

whip also called the slapstick, a special effects percussion instrument con-structed of two strips of wood, held together with a spring. When the two sides are slapped together, the sound imitates the crack of a whip. See also *percussion family.*

whistle a percussion instrument that produces a sharp whistling sound. Some varieties, like the tin whistle, can produce a number of different tones; others produce only a single tone. See also *percussion family.*

whole note the symbol representing a tone whose time value is equal to one full measure in 4/4 time. The whole tone (semibreve in English use) is the longest note value in modern use. See also *note; semibreve.*

---

whole note

---

whole rest a rest of time value equal to one full measure, regardless of meter. See also *rest.*

---

whole rest

whole tone   an interval of two half tones. The modern major and minor scales are distinguished by the placement of five whole tone intervals and two half tone intervals. Example: The major scale involves whole tones between each step except step 3 to 4, and step 7 to 8, which are half tones. See also *half step; interval; semitone.*

whole tone

half steps

whole-tone scale   a scale made up entirely of whole tone intervals, a division of the 12-tone scale into six segments of equal intervals. The whole-tone scale lacks the traditional and harmonically crucial intervals of a perfect fourth, perfect fifth, and minor second. See also *interval; perfect interval; scale.*

whole–tone scale

wind family   **(1)** instruments that produce sound by varying the size of a pipe while a column of air is forced through. The variation is achieved by opening or closing a series of holes or valves. Wind instruments use one of three types of mouthpieces: single reed (clarinet and saxophone); double reed (the oboe group); and the mouth hole (flute and piccolo). **(2)** in a broader application, all woodwind and brass instruments. See also *bassoon; clarinet; flute; oboe; piccolo; saxophone.*

wire brush   a type of drumstick with a head of stiff wires in place of wood or felt. It is used to create a subtle, soft sound on the suspended cymbal. See also *cymbal; drum; percussion family.*

wood block   hollow wooden percussion instruments of indefinite pitch, also called the Chinese or temple block. See also *Chinese block; percussion family; temple block.*

woodwind   any instrument in the wind family, including the piccolo, flute, oboe, clarinet, bassoon, recorder, and saxophone. The term "woodwind" is traditional but inaccurate, since the modern flute, piccolo, and saxophone are usually made of metal. And clarinets, oboes, and other woodwind instruments may be constructed of metal or plastic.

Woodwinds are characterized by six fingerholes or valves. Uncovering a hole or a series of holes raises the instrument's pitch. See also *wind family*.

wuchtig   (G.) forcefully.

X

xilofón   (Sp.) see *xylophone*.

xilofono   (It.) see *xylophone*.

xylophon   (G.) see *xylophone*.

xylophone   a definite pitch percussion instrument with wooden bars arranged in a keyboard like the piano. It is played with circular headed wooden mallets. The xylophone's range begins at middle C and extends upward for three octaves. Some versions have ranges beginning at F below middle C.

The wooden bars are attached by cord to a standing frame, and metal resonators are attached beneath the keyboard. See also *keyboard instrument; marimba; percussion family; vibraphone*.

xylophone

Z

zart   (G.) tenderly.

zarzuela   (Sp.) see *opéra comique*.

ziehharmonika (G.) see *accordion.*

zither a stringed instrument with up to 45 strings, each string representing a different tone. Strings are arranged in a wooden sound box. Individual strings may be stopped on a fretted board, while others are plucked. See also *string family.*

Multi-Language Instrument Guide

English	Italian	French	German	Spanish
Accordion	Accordeon	Accordéon	Ziehhar-monika	Acordeón
Alto Saxo-phone	Sassofono Contralto	Saxophone Alto	Altsaxo-phon	Saxo Alto
Alto Trom-bone	Trombone Contralto	Trombone Alto	Altposaune	Trombón Alto
Bagpipe	Cornamusa	Cornemuse	Dudelsack	Gaita
Baritone Saxophone	Sassofono Baritono	Saxophone Baryton	Bariton-saxophon	Saxo Barítono
Bass Drum	Gran Cassa	Grosse Caisse	Grosse Trommel	Gran Caja
Bass Saxo-phone	Sassofono Basso	Saxophone Basse	Bass-Saxo-phon	Saxo Bajo
Bass Trom-bone	Trombone Basso	Trombone Basse	Bass Posaune	Trombón Bajo
Bass Trum-pet	Tromba Bassa	Trompette Basse	Bass-trom-pete	Trompeta Baja
Basset Horn	Corno di Bassetto	Cor de Basset	Basset-horn	Corno di Bassetto
Bassoon	Fagotto	Basson	Fagott	Fagote
Bells	Campane	Cloches	Glocken	Campanas
Bongo	Bongo	Bongo	Bongo	Bongó
Bugle	Flicorno	Bugle	Signalhorn	Flisocorno
Castanets	Castag-nette	Castag-nettes	Castag-nettes	Castañueles
Celesta	Celesta	Célesta	Celesta	Celesta
Cello	Violon-cello	Violon-celle	Cello	Violon-chelo
Clarinet	Clarinetto	Clarinette	Klarinette	Clarinete

247

English	Italian	French	German	Spanish
Contra-bassoon	Contra-fagotto	Contre-basson	Kontra-fagott	Contra-fagote
Contra-bass-tuba	Contra-tuba	Contre-tuba	Kontra-basstuba	Contra-tuba
Cornet	Cornetta	Cornet	Klapp-hörnchen	Corneta
Cymbal	Piatti	Cymbale	Becken	Platillo
Double Bass	Contra-basso	Contre-basse	Kontra-bass	Contra-bajo
Drum	Tamburo	Tambour	Trommel	Tambor
English Horn	Corno Inglese	Cor Anglais	Englisch-horn	Corno Ingles
Euphonium	Eufonio	Euphonium	Euphonium	Eufonio
Fife	Piffeto	Fifre	Querpfeife	Flautín
Flageolet	Flautino	Flageolet	Flageolett	Caramillo
Flute	Flauto	Flûte	Flöte	Flauta
Glocken-spiel	Campanelli	Jeu de Timbres	Glocken-spiel	Campanelli
Gong	Gong	Gong	Gong	Gong
Guitar	Chitarra	Guitare	Gitarre	Guitarra
Harmonica	Armonica	Harmonica	Mundhar-monika	Armónica
Harmonium	Organetto	Harmonium	Harmonium	Armonio
Harp	Arpa	Harpe	Harfe	Arpa
Harpsi-chord	Claricem-balo	Clavecin	Cembalo	Clavecín
Log Drum	Tamburo di Legno	Tambour de Bois	Schlitz-trommel	Tambor de Madera
Lute	Liuto	Luth	Laute	Laúd
Lyre	Lira	Lyre	Leier	Lira
Mandolin	Mandolino	Mandoline	Mandola	Mandolina
Maracas	Maracas	Maracas	Maracas	Maracas
Marimba	Marimba	Marimba	Marimba	Marimba
Musical Saw	Sega	Scie Musi-cale	Musikal-ische Säge	Serrucho

English	Italian	French	German	Spanish
Oboe	Oboe	Hautbois	Oboe	Oboe
Organ	Organo	Orgue	Orgel	Organo
Piano	Pianoforte	Piano	Klavier	Piano
Piccolo	Flauto Piccolo	Petite Flûte	Piccolo Flöte	Piccolo Flautín
Rattle	Raganella	Crécelle	Klapper	Maraca
Recorder	Flauto a Becco	Flûte à Bec	Block-flöte	Flaute de Pico
Saxophone	Sassofono	Saxophone	Saxophon	Saxofón
Side Drum	Tamburo Militare	Tambour Militaire	Militär-trommel	Tambor Militar
Siren	Sirena	Sirène	Sirene	Sirena
Sleigh Bells	Sonagli	Grelots	Schellen	Cascabeles
Slide-Whistle	Sirena di Fischietto	Flûte à Coulisse	Schiebe Flöte	Sirena de Pico
Snare Drum	Cassa Chiara	Caisse Claire	Kleine Trommel	Caja Clara
Soprano Saxophone	Sassofono Soprano	Saxophone Soprano	Sopran-saxophon	Saxo So-prano
String Drum	Tamburo Frottato	Tambour à Friction	Reib-trom-mel	Tambor Frotado
Tam-Tam	Tam-Tam	Tam-Tam	Tam-Tam	Tam-Tam
Tambour-ine	Tamburo Basco	Tambour de Basque	Schellen-trommel	Tambor Vasco
Tenor Drum	Cassa Ru-lante	Caisse Rou-lante	Rollir-trommel	Caja Ro-lante
Tenor Sax-ophone	Sassofono Tenore	Saxophone Tenor	Tenorsax-ophon	Saxo Tenor
Tenor Trom-bone	Trombone Tenore	Trombone Ténor	Tenor-posaune	Trombón Tenor
Timpani	Timpani	Timbales	Pauke	Timbales
Tom-Tom	Tom-Tom	Tom	Tom	Tom
Triangle	Triangolo	Triangle	Triangel	Triangulo
Trombone	Trombone	Trombone	Posaune	Trombón
Trumpet	Tromba	Trompette	Trompete	Trompeta

English	Italian	French	German	Spanish
Tuba	Tuba	Tuba	Tuba	Tuba
Value Horn	Corno	Cor d'har-monie	Ventil-horn	corno
Vibraphone	Vibrafono	Vibraphone	Vibraphon	Vibráfono
Viola	Viola	Alto	Bratsche	Viola
Violin	Violono	Violon	Geige	Violín
Whip	Frusta	Fouet	Rute	Látigo
Whistle	Fischietto	Sifflet	Pfeife	Pito
Wood Block	Blocco di Legno	Bloc de Bois	Woodblock	Cocos
Xylophone	Xilofono	Xylophone	Xylophon	Xilofón

Illustrated Notation Guide

bar lines

1 between measures
2 end of score

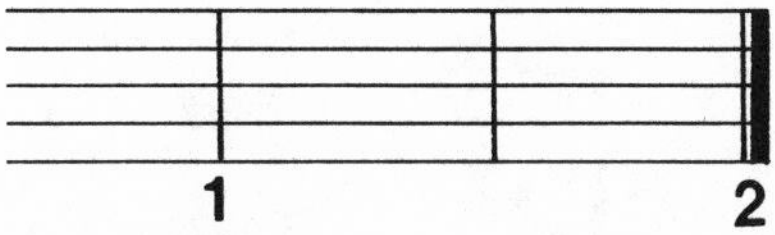

1   2

braces

2-staff instrument

**2-staff instrument
within an ensemble**

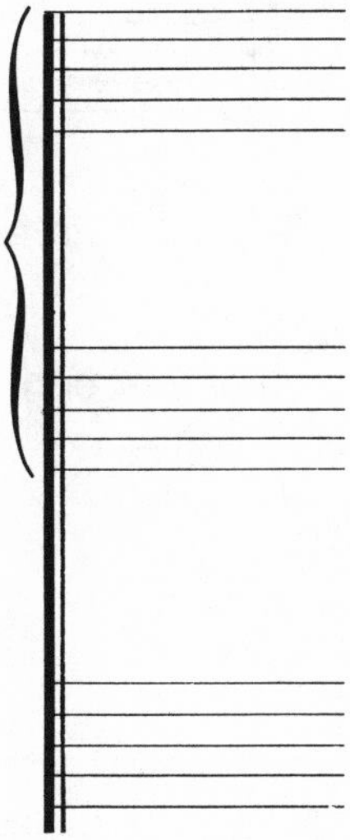

braces

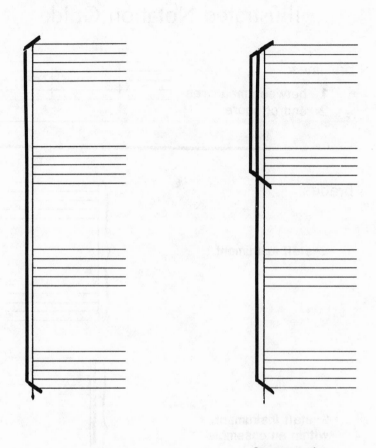

choir section

**2–part voice
within a choir
section**

clefs

treble

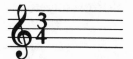

bass

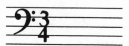

alto

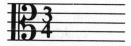

tenor

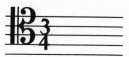

indefinite pitch

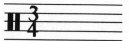

percussion

clef changes

key changes

**eliminated
accidentals**

**replaced
accidentals**

ledger lines

meter notation

meter

meter
changes

---

metronome mark

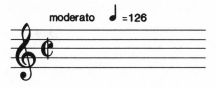

---

note types

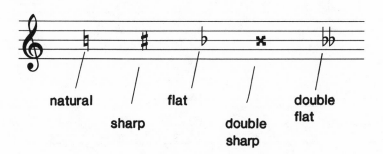

note values

whole

eighth
Flags   Beams

half

sixteenth

quarter

thirty-second

sixty-fourth

---

note values – variations

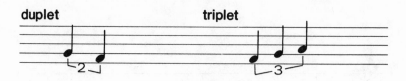

duplet

triplet

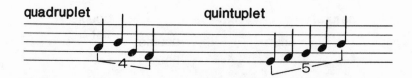

quadruplet

quintuplet

performance directions

accent	**arpeggio**
bowing down–bow up–bow	**fermata**
	glissando
harmonic	**legato**
marcato	**mordent**
pedal marks	**rehearsal marks**
	sforzando

performance directions

repeats

section

**section,
different
ending**

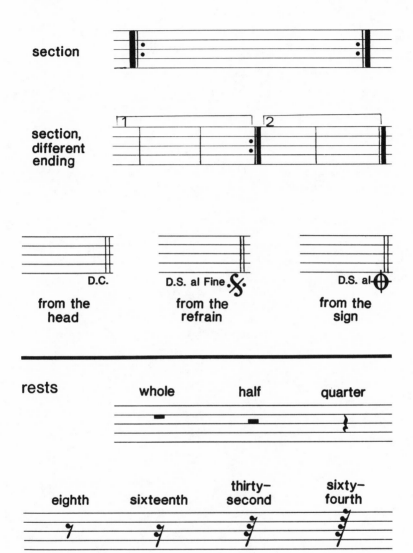

D.C.

**from the
head**

D.S. al Fine

**from the
refrain**

D.S. al

**from the
sign**

rests

whole   half   quarter

eighth   sixteenth   thirty-
second   sixty-
fourth

**multiple
measures**

Scales, Keys and Chords

major scales

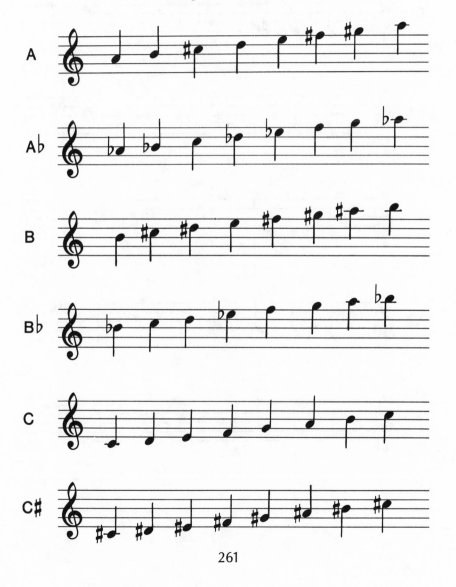

C♭

D

D♭

E

E♭

F

harmonic minor scales

E

E♭

F

F♯

G

G♯

melodic minor scales

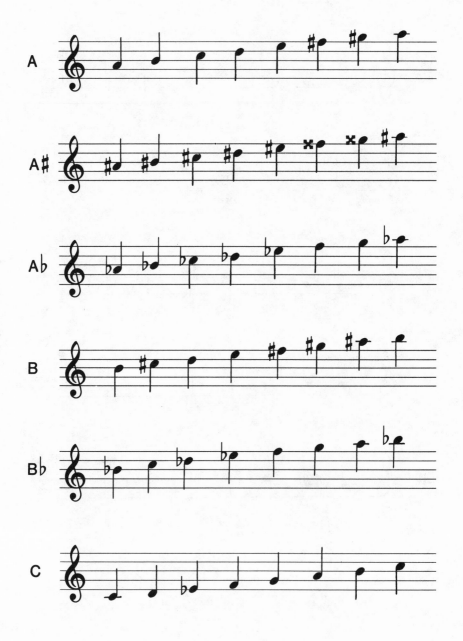

C#

D

D#

E

Eb

F

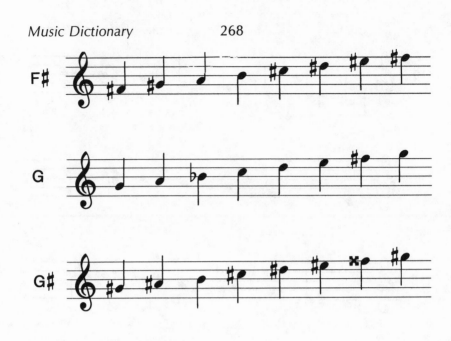

natural minor scales

B

B♭

C

C♯

D

D♯

E

E♭

F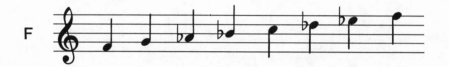

F♯

G

G♯

Church modes

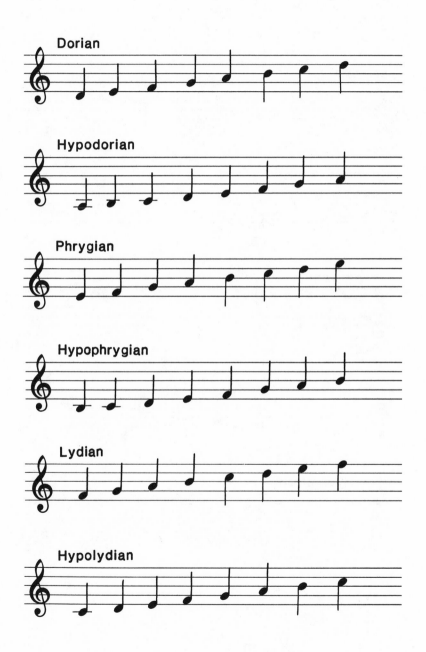

Mixolydian

Hypomixolydian

Aeolian

Hypoaeolian

Ionian

Hypoionian

key signatures

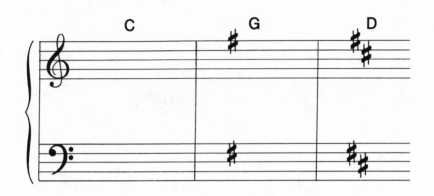

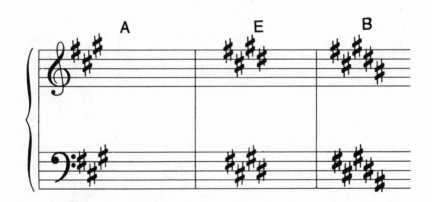

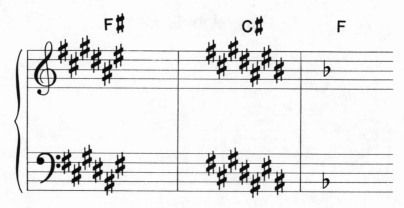

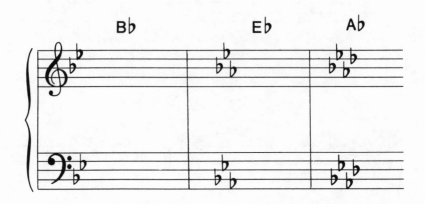

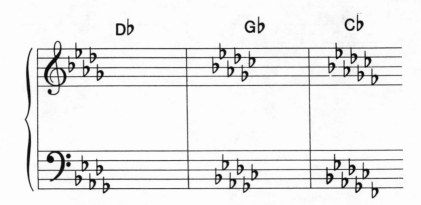

major chords

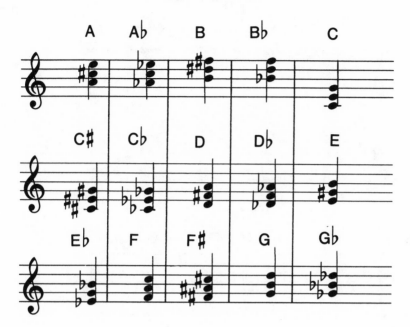

minor chords

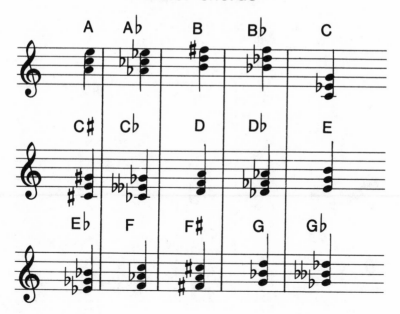

diminished chords

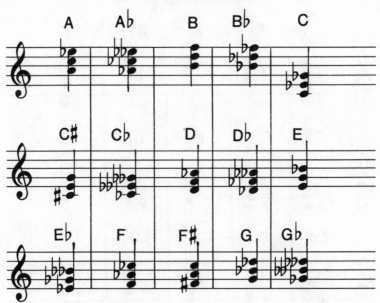

augmented chords

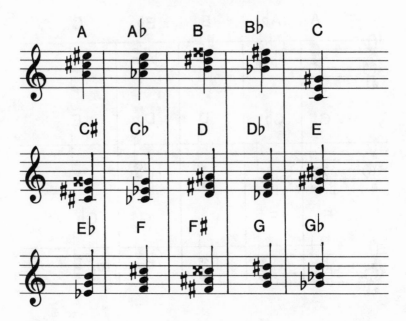

dominant seventh chords

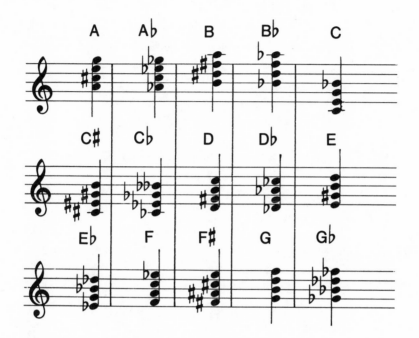